INTERNATIONAL

Hotel and Resort Design

INTERNATIONAL
Hotel and Resort Design

Anne M. Schmid & Mary Scoviak-Lerner

HOTELS
& RESTAURANTS INTERNATIONAL

PBC International, Inc. ■ New York

Distributor to the book trade in the United States and Canada:

Rizzoli International Publications, Inc.
597 Fifth Avenue
New York, NY 10017

Distributor to the art trade in the United States:

Letraset USA
40 Eisenhower Drive
Paramus, NJ 07653

Distributor to the art trade in Canada:

Letraset Canada Limited
555 Alden Road
Markham, Ontario L3R 3L5, Canada

Distributed throughout the rest of the world by:

Hearst Books International
105 Madison Avenue
New York, NY 10016

Library of Congress Cataloging-in-Publication Data

Schmid, Anne.
    The best of hotel and resort design.

    Includes indexes.
    1. Hotels, taverns, etc.   2. Resort architecture.
I.   Scoviak, Mary.   II. Title.
NA7800.S35   1988   728'.5   88-60876
ISBN 0-86636-068-9

CAVEAT--Information in this text is believed accurate, and will pose no problem for the student or casual reader. However, the authors were often constrained by information contained in signed release forms, information that could have been in error or not included at all. This refers specifically to the names of hotels, designers, management companies, architects and photographers. Any misinformation (or lack of information) in these areas is the result of failure in these attestations. The authors have done whatever is possible to insure accuracy.

Color separation, printing and binding by
Toppan Printing Co. (H.K.) Ltd. Hong Kong
Typesetting by **Jeanne Weinberg Typesetting**

10 9 8 7 6 5 4 3 2 1

ACKNOWLEDGEMENTS

In the preparation of this book, we are deeply indebted to Helga Albrecht, our diligent editorial assistant; our editor, Kevin Clark; our art directors, Richard Liu and Daniel Kouw; our consultant, Reinhold F. Schmid, president, Redesign, Inc.; and Dr. Robert M. Lerner (D. Litt.), whose editorial artistry and dedication made the writing and editing of this book possible.

STAFF

MANAGING DIRECTOR	*Penny Sibal-Samonte*
CREATIVE DIRECTOR	*Richard Liu*
FINANCIAL DIRECTOR	*Pamela McCormick*
ASSOCIATE ART DIRECTOR	*Daniel Kouw*
EDITORIAL MANAGER	*Kevin Clark*
ARTIST	*Kim McCormick*

Contents

Foreword

Whether the subject is an historic inn in Ireland, a sophisticated resort in the Caribbean or a tasteful business hotel in Singapore, there is a theme that unites the hotel designs in this handsome volume. All are the result of collaboration between an enlightened owner and a knowledgeable designer who work together to create a very special setting for a public that is becoming increasingly aware of its environment. The expressions of their cooperation are aesthetically pleasing works of art, yet not art for art's sake. These properties contain functionally correct spaces, carefully planned for human needs and comfort.

The artistic freedom and functional challenge inherent in hotel design make it one of the most rewarding of the design disciplines. Hotel designers must deal with differently sized public spaces, dining rooms and gathering places, lounges and ballrooms, shops and offices, and, most importantly, with residential areas. A hotel is a place where people live, for however short a time.

Designers face the task of creating a sense of theater in each of these aspects. They can shape the image of the hotel by dealing with emotional responses to the broad categories of form, shape, color, lighting and objects. But, at the same time, designers must pay close attention to details—often, thousands of details.

On the opening day of the glorious Ritz Hotel in Paris, Cesar Ritz, the greatest of hoteliers, discovered to his horror that the tables in the dining room were two centimeters too high. Within two hours of opening, he had them cut down to the correct height. Hotel designers live through these experiences many times in their careers because they understand that details play a significant role in the success of a hotel.

Though the basic goal of design remains constant, there can be no rubber stamp hotel design. As this book amply illustrates, hotels cover the spectrum from intimate jewel boxes to properties with more than 1,000 rooms covering entire city blocks. Hotels are used for different purposes: relaxation, conventions, business. Designers must create a specific background, much like a stage set, for each project.

Design cannot be done in a vacuum. It must reflect a setting, whether architectural or geographical. The ultimate experience for a hotel designer is to create an original environment using interesting forms and contemporary technology while working in the context of great architecture. Add to this a sense of place, be it China or New York, urban or seaside, the hotel is environment complete.

As this book demonstrates, the variety of design solutions is unlimited, both for new construction, for which designers must anticipate styles and shapes, or for restoration of worthwhile buildings, for which the designer must reach back to recreate old but still glorious themes.

The constant evolution of the hotel industry and increasing sophistication of travelers has sparked an explosion of appropriate themes and styles. It is no longer unthinkable to have Country French in California, Japanese in Mexico or Chicago, nautical in the city, urban on the seashore, Victorian in China, Contemporary California along the Rhine, British in Hong Kong, or New England in Laguna. These paradoxical approaches are delightful challenges for designers, and welcome changes for aesthetically-jaded guests.

Whatever approach designers take, they must keep in mind that they are designing for human beings—the guests. There is, most definitely, a social responsibility to hotel design. There is no other environment where so many people are exposed to contemporary interior design. Hotel design should help the general public become aware of design, as well as making people aware of both classical and modern levels of good taste. Hopefully, we designers of hotels who spend our lives in one of the most challenging yet rewarding of experiences, can be responsive to such needs.

Howard Hirsch

Often credited with revolutionizing the field of hotel design into a professional discipline, Howard Hirsch is the founder and senior partner of Hirsch/Bedner & Associates, headquartered in Santa Monica, California. Based on dollar volume, Hirsch/Bedner currently is the largest interior design firm in the world that specilizes in hotel design.

Hirsch, who studied art and design at Chicago's prestigious Art Institute and was graduated from the University of Paris (Sorbonne and Beaux Arts), founded his own firm in 1974 and began Hirsch/Bedner in 1979 when Michael Bedner became partner. The firm currently has offices in Atlanta and London, in addition to its Santa Monica headquarters, and a staff of 200 professionals.

Hirsch/Bedner's impact is felt worldwide on such varied projects as the 750-room Westin Maui and the 850-room Westin Kauai, both located in Hawaii; the 465-room Hyatt on Collins in Melbourne, Australia; and the 520-room Hyatt Regency Jerusalem. Other projects are underway in Australia, China, Hawaii, Hong Kong, Taipei and West Germany.

Introduction

For hundreds of years, hotels have been counted among the most beautiful buildings in the world.

It is therefore surprising that hotel design is such a young discipline. While it is true that some hoteliers of the 19th Century had an innate understanding of how to create effective and elegant interiors, it is equally true that, for many properties, real "design" ended with the architecture at the lobby, and the rest of the hotel was simply "decorated" using whatever money and furnishings that remained.

The days of pure "decoration" are over. Though the artistry remains, it has been painted with the logic of problem solving. Hotels are glamorous businesses, but they are businesses, nevertheless. Hotel designers are not building monuments to themselves, but multi-use environments that will be a home away from home for some, an office for others, and a site for entertainment or celebration for still more. The goal of the hotel designer's art is to forge a variety of shape, color and form into a memorable identity that will attract guests and make them want to return.

Though these constraints are undeniably challenging, they are balanced by the opportunity for almost unlimited creativity. As the hotel industry and its patrons become increasingly sophisticated, their tolerance for different types of design expands. At no time have owners and investors been more willing to take a step on to the leading edge, whether that means a sumptuously more-is-more rendition of opulent Victorian, or a bold—even avant-garde—prediction of 1990s modern. Good design gives a hotel a strong personality that promises personalized service. It addresses the demands of guests that hotels have standards without standardization.

The criteria for good design are as broad as the industry itself. As the examples in this book demonstrate, no single category of hotel has a monopoly on fine design. A six-room bed and breakfast lovingly restored on a small budget, can make as important a design statement as a mega-hotel renovated by the resources of a powerful hotel chain.

Nor does a hotel have to be traditionally "beautiful" to be aesthetically significant. The classic concept of "beauty," as applied to interiors, has very little to do with some of the hotels depicted in this volume. They deserve the labels of "exotic" or "daring." Some shatter the preconceived notion of how a hotel should look in every aspect, while others use details to reinterpret the expected and create a new language of design.

The themes that inspire these designs are equally broad, ranging from Renaissance villas to centers of high technology, or from spare, urban oases to the lush seclusions of tropical resorts. There is no one, "right" design answer for hotels. What is "right" is what is dictated by the architecture, cultural setting, and clientele.

More and more hotels reflect this understanding. Though not all the examples in this book were designed by professional interior designers or even described by those who submitted them in technical design terms, these interiors share an aesthetic completeness. They are comprehensive artistic environments in which lobby and guest room, corridor and board room, reflect the same intense attention to design.

Because the spectrum of hotel design is so broad, not every appealing property could be included in this single volume. Rather, the aim is to show a representative cross-section of thought-provoking design work that is influencing the present and future of the field.

Design must keep evolving with the hotel industry, now one of the most important industries in the world. Renovation and restoration help to insure that designers will keep looking for new solutions. The investment required to build a hotel—sometimes upward of US$300 million—mandates that the days of "bulldoze and build again" are gone.

In many European city centers, only grande dame hotels are old enough to have prime sites. These are the properties that preserve pieces of civilizations. Their restoration is as much a matter of social concern as of financial necessity. Yet, they must be rejuvenated if they are to continue.

Hotels built in the last 20 years must undergo renovation if they are to meet the challenges posed by new hotels seeking to steal their markets. Few things turn away loyal customers as much as outdated furnishings, scratched casegoods or napless carpets that—to the guests—are synonymous with an overall lack of concern about the property.

The hotel industry is highly competitive and, as many hotel companies follow their clients around the world, it can only become more competitive. Hoteliers must use all the tender traps at their disposal to lure out and maintain their client base. A good measure of their success is determined by the quality of their service. But it is also determined by the design. How a hotel looks tells guests what to expect—how deluxe it is, how large it is, or even where it is. For example, marble surfaces are not installed for the sake of art. They are beautiful, but they also tell guests they are in a top-rate, deluxe environment.

Hotel design is similar to classic forms of art. It uses visual elements to create an image that evokes a response. But it is different than painting or sculpting because it demands a response—a decision to register or dine, a commitment to return. That is what makes hotel design unique and fascinating. It is also what helps insure that hotels, the most private of public buildings, will continue to set standards of aesthetic excellence.

Mary Scoviak-Lerner
Editor, Hotels & Restaurants International

CHAPTER 1

Five-Star Hotels

Richard Callen

Trisha Wilson

Werner Aeberhard

*I*n the jargon of the hotel industry, "5 star" means, quite simply, the best—in service, cuisine and design.

Though much of the formality once synonymous with this stellar status has disappeared along with other aspects of social rigidity, the requirement that these stars of the hotel world wrap their guests in luxury remains.

In hotel design terms, elegance and luxury are unexpectedly broad concepts. They can apply to a dramatically monochromatic lobby with clean-lined contemporary furnishings as aptly as to an opulent grande dame, colored in jewel tones and dressed out in rich mahogany and marble. Today's 5-star hotels can include exotic local crafts alongside priceless antiques or laser lights in a disco contrasted with crystal chandeliers in the lobby. But, whatever the mix, the message must be uniform: top quality.

As Werner Aeberhard, London-based principal of Wilson Gregory Aeberhard puts it, "The standards of 5-star facilities should be the same anywhere in the world, as should the level of detailing. But the materials, design elements and geometrics must change to relate to the culture and the setting."

Trisha Wilson, US-based principal of Wilson Gregory Aeberhard and also principal of Dallas-based Wilson and Associates, adds, "A 5-star hotel must utilize a higher quality of materials including the millwork, furnishings, carpeting and artwork. The bathroom, in particular, has become a quality center in 5-star hotels. We are seeing upgraded standards in terms of a separate shower, a soaking tub, extra large vanities with plenty of room to unpack toiletries and extra dollars being spent on vanity lighting."

"The dramatic blend of architectural detailing, appropriate furnishings, unique art and artifacts often indigenous to the locale, special lighting and exquisite guest amenities all combine in 5-star hotels to enhance the feeling of inviting, luxurious comfort," says Richard Callen, president of Intra-design, headquartered in the USA. "Not unlike designing the interior of a grand residence, hotel design must create an elegant and intimate, yet functional accommodation for today's sophisti-cated and eclectic hotel clientele."

FOUR SEASONS HOTEL

Location: LOS ANGELES, CALIFORNIA, USA
Hotel Company: FOUR SEASONS HOTELS LTD.
Interior Design: INTRADESIGN
Architecture: GIN WONG ASSOCIATES
Photography: JAIME ARDILES-ARCE

Los Angeles glitters. The Four Seasons Hotel in Los Angeles glows, washed in a decidedly un-Californian palette of black, gray and honeyed gold played against marble surfaces and rich custom millwork.

Housed in a 16-story translation of a French chateau, this 285-room property features a residentially eclectic mix of European antiques, American contemporary art and Chinese accents that is visually exciting yet elegant enough for a truly deluxe hotel bordering posh Beverly Hills.

Designers with California-based Intradesign established this luxurious residential theme in the lobby. The registration area was scaled down and the elevator corridor was shifted to one side to eliminate the lineup of guests and baggage that constrict the traffic flow through many hotels. Instead of punctuating the lobby with random seating, Intradesign integrated a mix of French-inspired furnishings into a "living room" adjacent to the registration area where guests can linger undisturbed.

This residential theme is carried through to the dining areas where arched Palladian windows offer clear views of the beautifully landscaped grounds. The designers also subdivided the large space set aside for the dining areas to create a more intimate, even private, dining experience.

Guest rooms, too, reflect the hotel's commitment to quality. They feature marble-topped desks, exotic accent veneers for maple cabinets and, in some cases, canopy beds. Four different color schemes, ranging from soft tones to rust, gray and beige, mean that repeat guests can enjoy a different experience each time they visit the hotel.

An elegant marble bust framed by an antique tapestry mixes with fine reproductions to create a rich yet relaxed appeal in the "Living Room."

Classically-inspired French chairs serve as softening counterpoints to the sleek, contemporary lines of the concierge's desk. Accents are minimal but effective: a blush of color from a small floral arrangement, a note of elegance in the ornate picture frame.

Arches of the hotel's signature Palladian windows are reflected in the entry to the Garden Restaurant.

Deep brown walls enhance a rich wood oval table in the private dining room of the Four Seasons. Though the chandelier adds design drama, warm, subtle, recessed lighting ensures the entire room will have even illumination.

HOTEL
DE L'EUROPE

Location: AMSTERDAM, NETHERLANDS
Interior Design: MAURICE GROTHAUSEN
Architecture: MAURICE GROTHAUSEN

With historical roots that link it to Amsterdam's first inn built in 1683 within the sturdy walls of a fort, the Hotel de l'Europe has faced continual challenges to earn and maintain its 5-star status.

Ongoing refinement of the hotel's interiors is an essential part of this process. One of the major difficulties facing designer and architect Maurice Grothausen of Amsterdam in the most recent renovation was to provide modern conveniences necessary to a 5-star ranking without sacrificing elements of historical importance or aspects characteristic of the hotel.

Architectural moldings and other details synonymous with a more than 100-year-old building like the Hotel de l'Europe can be used to mask the introduction of modern ventilation and climate control systems.

Grothausen also had to address the varied shapes of the hotel's 80 guest rooms and 20 suites. By keeping to pale color schemes, he visually expanded even smaller rooms. Fabrics share a basic color, but offer an interesting diversity of texture and pattern.

The major exception to this classic palette can be found in Le Cafe, where wood paneled walls and deep colors create a snug refuge after a hectic business day.

Whether in public spaces or guest rooms, the designer selected low-line furnishings for a classical human scale but broke this horizontal line by drawing visual interest upward with elegant crystal chandeliers and traditional ceiling accents.

Innovative design transforms a room into a suite. An amply-draped architectural pavilion effectively creates a separate "bedroom," while a plush sofa and chairs in the same color values provide functional living space.

Modern bathrooms are musts especially for historic 5-star hotels. Gleaming marble surfaces and gold-toned fixtures lend an unmistakable luxury.

HOTEL SHILLA

Location: SEOUL, KOREA
Interior Design: ARTIPLAN; KANKO KIKAKU SEKKEISHA;
     OGAWA FERR-DUTHILLEUL: TOTAL INTEGRATED;
     SAM WOO ARCHITECTURAL & ENGINEERING CO.;
     DAI SEI CONSTRUCTION
Architecture: SAMSUNG CONSTRUCTION CO., LTD.

Korea's ancient Shilla Dynasty, a period during which art and culture flourised, provides both the spiritual and aesthetic inspiration for the 640-room Hotel Shilla.

Pristinely modern on the exterior, the hotel's interior combines the high points of Korea's artistic past with the modern necessities required in a world-class hotel. The lobby is crowned by golden chandeliers modeled on the resplendent belts worn by the Kings of the Shilla Dynasty, which lasted from 57 B.C. to 935 A.D. Sculpted into the lobby walls are ornamental relief patterns, called "wadang," which recall historic Korean renderings of the lotus flower. Even the sloping ceiling of the lobby and its octagonal columns are reminders of the dynasty that celebrated a united Korean peninsula.

Six design firms representing France, Japan, Korea and Singapore collaborated on the interiors of the hotel, which is set amidst 23 acres of wooded gardens. The designers brought that peaceful feeling into the hotel's guest rooms by choosing furnishings with horizontal lines and limiting strong accents to a single focus: an undulating floral upholstery fabric, an exquisitely carved wooden screen or armoire, or a quietly beautiful painting.

Yet, because this 15-year-old hotel attracts a highly international clientele, the hotel also offers several suites decorated in classic French style, correct in every detail from gilded chair frames to columns with ornate Corinthian capitals and Empire accents.

Necessary casegoods are elevated to works of art in the intricately-carved wooden furnishings and room dividers used to define the Korean Suite.

From the shell-capped wall niches to the wreath motif on the desk and gilded chairs, Hotel Shilla's Presidential Suite faithfully recalls the accents of the French Empire period.

The grid-like design of the wall panels, reflected in the ceiling and carpeting, creates classically appealing proportions for the 94-seat Sorabol restaurant.

LAS HADAS

Location: MANZANILLO, MEXICO
Hotel Company: WESTIN HOTELS & RESORTS
Interior Design: VALERIAN RYBAR; FRANCOIS COIROUS;
JEAN PAUL OLIVIER
Architecture: EZQUERRA Y ASOCIADOS, S.A.

The "vital statistics" profiling Mexico's fabled Las Hadas resort list no founder, only an "original visionary": the late Bolivian tin magnate, Don Antenor Patino. He assigned a team of architects and interior designers to give his vision shape and substance, and make it "the most unique resort in the world."

Ten years and US$33 million later, in 1974, Las Hadas opened. Every detail of this 220-room property adds to the fantasy environment: from its bleached white Moorish turrets and crenelated walls, to its spacious and airy guest rooms. The white-on-white theme set by the startling exteriors is carried into the guest rooms, where white stucco walls—often rounded or linked by graceful arches—flow into white marble floors to create a complete yet otherworldly environment.

Against this cool backdrop, designers worked with varieties of color and texture. Fabric accents draped from some guest room ceilings offer a softer interpretation of architectural moldings. Wicker furnishings serve as textural counterpoint to the smooth floors. While some rooms use monochromatic schemes punctuated only by bright, fresh flowers picked from the hotel grounds, others introduce clear pastels: blue-greens, bright yellows, cool peaches. Accessories are minimized in order to accentuate the cool, calming atmosphere of this resort.

Three of the hotel's four dining areas take advantage of a virtually perfect climate, allowing guests to dine on terraces or have views of the pool. Areas of the terrace are tiled to provide visual interest, while palm trees throughout shade diners and give each table a feeling of privacy.

Gleaming white walls and spiraling mosque-like towers endow Las Hadas with an undeniable look of fantasy.

Curving arches and the play of different textures make the Presidential Suite reminiscent of a room from The Arabian Nights. This special suite is located in a separate building and has its own pool and terrace.

A monochromatic color scheme, accented with a burst of colors from fresh flowers supplied daily, adds drama to the Las Hadas Suite, a favorite of the resort's "original visionary," Don Antenor Patino.

Palm trees serve as natural dividers to give diners in the El Palmar restaurant a sense of privacy without obstructing their view of the laguna pool.

GRAND BAY HOTEL

A mix of natural materials with eye-catching antiques and floral accents creates a look of tropical elegance that defines the Grand Bay, whether in the lobby or the guest rooms and suites.

Location: COCONUT GROVE, FLORIDA, USA
Hotel Company: CONTINENTAL COMPANIES
Interior Design: JEFFREY HOWARD ASSOCIATES;
DIANA S. SEPLER INTERIORS
REGINE'S INTERIORS
Architecture: THE NICHOLAS PARTNERSHIP
Photography: DAN FORER

An unexpected mix of Mayan architecture, Old World antiques and suites that reflect cultures from Chinese to African create visual excitement in the Grand Bay Hotel.

This two-time winner of the prestigious Mobil Travel Guide 5-Diamond designation, offered Florida designers Jeffrey Howard Associates and Diane S. Sepler Interiors, a series of challenges.

"One of the major problems we faced was sun control," said Jeffrey Howard, who created designs for the hotel's public space.

To solve this problem without eliminating window space, Howard turned to natural materials: stucco walls thick enough to keep interiors bright and cool, and ample landscaping to screen out the hot southern Florida sun without closing off the view.

Despite its avant-garde architecture, the interiors are opulently traditional. Gone are the block-long registration desks. Grand Bay guests register at antique wooden desks in private areas lighted by two chandeliers adjacent to the main entry corridor.

Natural woods and cool brass carry this look into the hotel's restaurants and lounge. Seating encompasses an eclectic spectrum from leather to plush fabric to cane, with colors ranging from soft sands to almost shocking pinks.

Sepler rooted guest room design in a classic French country theme, which meant that light colors and patterns could be used for maximum effect. The departure from this scheme is in the hotel's one-of-a-kind theme suites where the furnishings could recall an African safari, the caliphate splendor of Marakesh, or the serenity of a Chinese pagoda.

Contrast warm colors with
cool surfaces and the result is
the upbeat, Old World charm
of the Ciga bar, named for
the ultra-deluxe Italian Ciga
Hotel chain. Grand Bay is
Ciga's first affiliate in the USA.

CAPITAL HILTON HOTEL

Location: WASHINGTON, D.C.
Hotel Company: HILTON HOTELS CORP.
Interior Design: HUGHES DESIGN ASSOCIATES
Architecture: ADD, INC.
Photography: JAIME ARDILES-ARCE

A "colonnade" of trees brings the sight line of the Capital Hilton's lobby to a more human scale but preserves the traditional formality reflected in the facing cherry columns.

Hughes Design Associates had one year to transform a tired hotel still clinging to World War II era design into a glamorous Hilton flagship.

Though the hotel had to remain open during the renovation, its interiors had been virtually gutted, giving designer Pamela Hughes the freedom to design an impressive, club-like lobby with a traditional appeal appropriate for its Washington, D.C. Setting.

She brought the front desk from an obscure location in the rear of the lobby to a highly-visible position. Traditional cherry was used for columns and other millwork. However, to keep the lobby from becoming oppressively museum-like or static, Hughes selected furnishings with rounded contemporary lines, married to the traditional columns with rich cherry and cocoa upholstery fabrics for chairs, and deep florals for sofas.

The lobby bar also was rescued from dingy obscurity. Moving the bar into the lobby area made it more visible to hotel guests and added a sense of activity.

Restaurant space also required rethinking. Instead of sectioning off a number of small spaces, Hughes used one large space but effectively created two distinct restaurant areas through her design. Twigs Veranda has a light, open airy feeling while its counterpart, Twigs Grill, uses a dark, rich look typical of a posh club. A transitional seating area between the two can accommodate overflow seating or a Sunday brunch buffet.

Strong architectural elements provide dramatic space definition in the lobby, helping to establish the club-like atmosphere appropriate for a deluxe Washington, D.C. hotel.

THE RITZ-CARLTON, LAGUNA NIGUEL

Location: LAGUNA NIGUEL, CALIFORNIA, USA
Hotel Company: RITZ CARLTON
Interior Design: FRANK NICHOLSON, INC.
Architecture: WIMBERLY, WHISENAND, ALLISON, TONG & GOO

Art can be a focal point of hotels, but few properties have elevated it to the signature status as has the Ritz Carlton in Laguna Niguel.

Since this deluxe hotel's clientele is comprised of sophisticated international travelers, the blend of art and antiques is intentionally broad. Bronze sculptured dolphins by California artist John Edward Svenson are the centerpiece of a fountain near the entry.

Designer Frank Nicholson loosely based the hotel's decor on that of a Mediterranean villa, since the rocky promontory on which the hotel sits is reminiscent of the French Riviera. This allowed him to establish different motifs in different areas, all unified by the focus on art, antiques and finishes.

He used a pair of paintings depicting British ships at sea by Dominic Serres, The Elder, to set a maritime theme in an area which opens onto a panoramic view of the Pacific Ocean. This maritime mood continues in the bar, featuring work by such British ship portraitists as Thomas Whitecombe, Thomas Lunch and William Howard York.

The villa theme enabled Nicholson to depart from this maritime motif for the formal dining room, done in candlelight neutrals and accented by French Provincial chandeliers. As in most traditional French restaurants, the decor is elegant, but restrained to provide a quiet backdrop for the food which takes center stage.

English, French and Spanish styles are represented in the 16 conference rooms of this 393-room hotel, which draws the carriage trade of conference business. From the English cut-crystal chandeliers and 19th Century French Napoleon III Aubusson tapestries in the ballroom, to the scenes of Venice by 19th and early 20th century English and Spanish painters, conference and function rooms are designed to reflect an aura of artistic elegance.

Modeled after a Mediterranean villa, the Ritz Carlton's design is tailored to space and function requirements: whether a light, airy lounge (left) or a glowing, wooded library.

HILTON AT SHORT HILLS

Location: SHORT HILLS, NEW JERSEY, USA
Hotel Company: HILTON HOTELS CORP.
Interior Design: KENNETH E. HURD & ASSOC.
Architecture: THE GRAD PARTNERSHIP
Photography: ED JACOBY

Good taste is always appealing—a maxim proven by the Hilton at Short Hills.

Kenneth Hurd and his staff had to create tasteful design that balances its appeal between power shoppers, who selected the hotel because of its proximity to neighboring Bloomingdale's, and upscale business travelers, who required the latest in business and conference services.

Adding to the demands on Hurd's design was the fact that the hotel lies in an affluent gateway community that links high-energy eastern New Jersey with the country estates in the western part of the state.

"The client mix mandated that the interiors be elegant but not stuffy or formal," explained Hurd.

To open up even windowless spaces, Hurd created ceiling accents which draw attention upward. In some areas, he installed graceful chandeliers; on others, he used ceiling murals, as in the Terrace Cafe, or faux ceilings, as in the arches of The Greenhouse restaurant.

The building's architecture also posed challenges. As an example, the grand stairway traverses a 22-foot drop to the ballroom and conference level. Hurd played up its grandeur to fill the space and disguise the steep drop, but also visually dissected the distance by incorporating a mezzanine landing.

Pattern on pattern design lends residential appeal to the suites of the Hilton Short Hills.

Attention to detail, including the fabric on the chairbacks, the china in the hutch, and the beautifully-carved harp, make this dining area elegant yet comfortable.

A swimming pool is transformed into a Roman bath, thanks to a formal colonnade and the softly lighted arched ceiling.

RAMADA HOTEL ISTANBUL

Location:	ISTANBUL, TURKEY
Hotel Company:	RAMADA, INC.
Interior Design:	MIM-AR MIMARLIK LTD. SIRKETI; CASSINA CONTRACT DIVISION
Architecture:	ERTUNGA

The oldest concrete buildings in Turkey designed by a native architect, provided shelter to Istanbul's homeless and low-income families until the late 1970s. By then, even generous donations from the Turkish Flyers Foundation and other private sources proved insufficient to keep the more than 65-year-old buildings in adequate repair.

However, the Net Group of Companies saw a way to preserve this piece of the city's past. Through an ingenious architectural plan which linked the four apartment buildings under skylighted arcades, the buildings received new life as the town center's first five-star hotel.

None of the interior layouts was changed, nor was the facade altered. Under the watchful review of the Turkish Fine Arts Commission, the property's interiors focused on intricate Turkish patterns and the jewel tones of amethyst and quartz. Glass and water create a constant theme for the hotel, which includes waterfalls, streams and fountains.

All of the hotel's nine communal areas are filled with light, creating a synthesis between the interior and exterior environments.

The area which links the buildings goes beyond a simple point of convergence to become a miniature community, complete with food and beverage outlets that resemble streetside cafes.

Skylighted arcades join the four historically important buildings that make up the Ramada Hotel, the first 5-star property in Istanbul's town center.

THE WATERFORD HOTEL

Location:	OKLAHOMA CITY, OKLAHOMA, USA
Interior Design:	INDEX THE DESIGN FIRM; BORDELON & ASSOCIATES
Architecture:	THE ARCHITECTURAL COMPENDIUM
Photography:	ROBERT MILLER

The Waterford Hotel wants to make its guests feel at home, not only through its caring service, but also through its design.

Designers sectioned off the hotel into major "living areas": The lobby is the parlor, the ballroom is the grand hall, and the Veranda dining room is the sunfilled morning room. These terms received more than lipservice, as the design team worked to keep the furnishings and art elements very residential in scale.

A row of 15-foot arched windows brightens the Veranda, for example. To eliminate any hint of institutional design, the team selected white wicker furnishings set against verde marble floors edged in Granada peach marble.

Even the lobby holds to the residential theme. Two semi-circular writing desks, which replace the more expected stand-up front desk, are paired with Hepplewhite arm chairs.

Designers for this award-winning hotel used details to carry this concept throughout the interior. Particular attention was paid to accents such as traditional moldings for the cove, base and chair rails, and custom-inset carpets, to make the interiors consistent.

A white oval island provides an interesting foundation for the breakfast buffet, which breaks up the long, narrow configuration of the Veranda dining room.

Despite the massive bar, the club room takes on a residential feel through the use of rich materials such as mahogany paneling and oak floors.

Traditional wood furnishings, such as armoires, are offset by vibrant floral fabrics in the 200 guest rooms of the Waterford Hotel.

HOTEL QUEEN ELIZABETH

Location: MONTREAL, CANADA
Hotel Company: CANADIAN PACIFIC
Interior Design: SK DESIGN INTERNATIONAL LTD.
Architecture: SK DESIGN INTERNATIONAL LTD.;
MARIUS BOUCHARD
Photography: PIERRE ZABBAL

Once described by a Montreal restaurant critic as "a pedestrian, impersonal, workhorse cafe," Le Montrealais in the Queen Elizabeth Hotel is now winning rave reviews for its innovative design.

Because it functions as a three-meal-a-day restaurant which attracts both hotel guests and local residents, its design must be as appealing for early morning breakfasters as for late night snackers. Designer Walter Schaepper, principal of SK Design, used an Italian bistro design to create a stylish but informal restaurant.

A complete refurbishment erased the tired 1960s style, with its standard mix of booths and low-back chairs. Instead, the designer added warm and intimate touches appropriate for an Italian bistro: marbled columns and arches—both straight-lined and gently curved—and deep, almost Renaissance colors like olive and red, cooled by a creamy beige, and rich wood accents.

Schaepper used planters and pillars to break up the large space essential to a restaurant which serves this 900-room conference hotel. A greenhouse facade adds an open air feeling to the bistro setting. In all, the project took seven months to complete.

Renaissance colors, dramatic architecture and wood accents result in an exciting design menu for what was once a tired 1960s coffee shop.

The gentle curves of painted chandeliers complement the rounded arches of the Le Montrealais Cafe. Particular attention too is paid to the tasteful wood and glass case used for a surprisingly elegant salad bar.

REGENT OKINAWA

Location: OKINAWA, JAPAN
Hotel Company: REGENT INTERNATIONAL
Interior Design: MEDIA FIVE LIMITED
Architecture: MEDIA FIVE LIMITED

There is nothing austere about the less-is-more approach used to create the dramatic, contemporary interiors of the 145-room Regent Okinawa.

The quality reflected in each aspect of the furniture and fixtures expands their impact beyond their individual shapes and styles to achieve a chic but not trendy elegance that updates the 1930s.

"We wanted a design approach that would be timeless—high quality, classic and not at all trendy," pointed out Tom Pagliuso, partner in charge of the Pacific based design firm, Media Five Limited.

In the lobby, the designers used a distinctive bullnose marble front desk to set the quality theme, and accented it with a sweeping marble and brass staircase, marble tables, custom area rugs and antique Okinawan artwork and crafts. Though the lobby is modestly sized when compared with many modern hotels, the importance of these design pieces lends it an approachable stateliness.

Pagliuso adds that the color scheme was purpsoely limited to neutrals to keep the interiors from looking dated in years to come.

This nod toward lasting quality continues in the bedrooms. Headboards and nightstands, which can quickly date a room, were eliminated in favor of a continuous ledge that runs along the bed wall. The color palette is comprised of relaxing beiges and slate blues. Suite schemes expand into soft grays and paler blues played against mauve accents.

Bold geometric lines and high quality materials result in strong, timeless design in both the public spaces and guest rooms of the deluxe Regent Okinawa.

KINSHASA INTERNATIONAL

Location: KINSHASA, ZAIRE
Hotel Company: INTER-CONTINENTAL HOTELS
Interior Design: WILSON GREGORY AEBERHARD
Photography: ROBERT MILLER

When conceptualizing the 250-room extension for the Inter-Continental Kinshasa, designers with Wilson Gregory Aeberhard had to consider that the hotel is a major meeting point in a modern and cosmopolitan African city. Yet, they could not "internationalize" its interiors so much that guests would lose a sense of place.

The result is a dynamic meshing of globally accepted 5-star design elements. For example, the lobby's glistening European crystal chandeliers are complemented by materials found in Africa and locally-made furnishings.

As another example, the marble lobby floor is inlaid with brilliant green malachite—a local mineral affordable in Zaire but expensive in other parts of the world. A large cast bronze sculpture loosely based on a human torso was created by a local artist to be a center-piece for the lobby. The reception desk has legs stylized to represent an African elephant's head and trunk, as do the desk chair and side chair.

Though vivid colors are used as accents, the quiet, creamy marble used for much of the lobby's surfaces offers a clean, crisp refreshing space away from the intense humidity of the outdoors. Selection of fabrics, finishes and furnishings had to be made with the climate in mind.

Because of the weather, the marble tops on tables in the Atrium Cafe were more necessity than luxury. Marble can withstand the climatic challenge and is decorative enough to eliminate the need for high-maintenance tablecloths.

Vivid colors cooled by neutral marble make the hotel's lobby a refreshing haven from Kinshasa's heat and humidity, while an explosive mix of hot colors on a black background turn up the energy in l'Atmosphere, one of Africa's most sophisticated discos.

PENINSULA HOTEL
NEW YORK

Location: NEW YORK, NEW YORK, USA
Hotel Company: THE PENINSULA GROUP
Interior Design: HIRSCH/BEDNER & ASSOCIATES
Architecture: AI GROUP/ARCHITECTS
Photography: JAIME ARDILES-ARCE

Hotel designers must cope not only with fast-paced schedules, but also a fast-paced industry. Hotels are bought and sold daily, which places added pressure on the designer to create interiors that belies no signature of a particular company's style.

Such was the case with the former Gotham Hotel in New York City. It had barely completed a renaissance that transformed it into the elegant Maxim's de Paris when it was purchased by the Hong Kong-based Peninsula Group.

Fortunately, designers from Hirsch/ Bedner formulated an Art Nouveau interior style that complemented the hotel's architecture. The spaces lent themselves to a Belle Epoque ambience realized through a combination of exquisite original pieces and charming reproductions.

Howard Hirsch used the sinuous, natural lines integral to the Art Nouveau style throughout the hotel—from the frames of the furnishings to the graceful twin curves of the grand staircase in the Hall d' Entree. "Anyone who walks into this hotel will feel like a character in a romantic play," he observes.

The hotel is a visual fantasyland of crystal chandeliers and handmade French carpets, handcarved tables and carefully upholstered wall panels. Its grand spaces permit this kind of opulence without edging into excess.

A single, stunning statue becomes a focal point for a quiet area warmed by polished wood and cheered with bright flowers.

Cascading down from formal, squared archways, the hotel's grand staircase sweeps into a lobby filled with warm woods and accented by a breathtaking crystal chandelier.

Guest room styles remain faithful to the Belle Epoque theme, from the elegant curves of the headboard to the balloon shades and cast bronze lamps.

Few characters embody the
style and spirit of the opulent,
sometimes excessive, Belle
Epoque than the divine Sarah
Bernhardt whose portrait
reigns over the hotel's public
spaces.

CHAPTER **2**

Historic Inns

Ann Richardson   R.J. Moyle

*O*nce upon a time most weary travelers rested in country inns, whether they were Richard the Lion-Hearted drinking mead and planning the rescue of England, or Athos, Porthos and Aramis sipping wine and waiting to be rounded up by D'Artignon.

A privileged few, the King Johns and Cardinal Richelieus, stayed in small, elite hotels that catered to the rich, powerful sophisticates.

"Age has afforded them (country inns and small hotels) time to develop an identity," says Ann Richardson, president of CSA Inc. of Minneapolis, Minnesota, "Their survival indicates their quality, charm, and even contribution to the environment."

She stresses the good economic news for owners. "The traveler who frequents the (country inns) seldom demands truly antique furnishings. He does, however, want authentic replication, (not) country French with Williamsburg with Art Deco."

From Great Britain, whose historic inns are the world's most copied, R.J. Moyle, design director of London's Tavern Furnishing Ltd. observes: "The larger hotels often try to emulate the smaller . . . but they never achieve the same degree of personal service. You are designing for someone who is investing his own money. The owner is more involved. . . he is far more concerned with details in every department."

Moyle contrasts this with purchasing directors of major hotel groups who are more concerned with bottom line figures, "which dictate that the majority of rooms are furnished in a similar style, (in turn) dictated by the maintenance that has to be carried out by housekeeping."

Not always, though, America's Richardson has the thought of "qualified standardization," which means ". . . colorways and patterns may vary, but compatibility is important so that pieces can be interchanged as properties age and replacements are required."

STAPLEFORD PARK

Location: LEICESTERSHIRE, ENGLAND
Interior Design: SLOANE DECORATORS
Architecture: BOB WEIGHTON

Strict old Queen Victoria wouldn't let her son, Edward, Prince of Wales, buy Stapleford Park. She feared his morals might be corrupted by the Leicestershire hunting society.

So today, this essentially 16th century wonderwork of architecture is a lodge, a country inn so voluptuous that famous designers each took over a single bedroom: Nina Campbell, Jane Churchill, Crabtree & Evelyn, Tiffany & Co., Wedgewood . . .

It took one year for Bob Payton, famed London restaurateur, to have readied his 30 bedrooms and six public rooms. Each room has a separate personality, yet regardless of the differences in design, fabric and furnishings, each room belongs in a historic manor house.

This is how the "landed gentry" lived, with marble staircases and glorious murals, fireplaces and four-posters. There are even the inevitable Merino sheep grazing on the lawn, adding a touch of class.

Putting 21st century technology into a building first mentioned in the Domesday Book, without sacrificing its history, was the toughest part of the project.

Stapleford Park is history, a history carefully nurtured by British designers, coordinated by Annie Charlton, who performed their work with an amazing sense of responsibility.

If Edward were to step inside today, he'd buy it without asking his mother.

This Crabtree & Evelyn baronial bedroom features swagged curtains and clustered paintings to emphasize height and lend historic accuracy. A marbled and arched bathroom focuses on a trompe l'oeil mural that looks into the clean countryside.

The Lady Gretton bedroom is unbelievably bright in classic green, a color often used centuries ago in manor houses. The bright reds and purples also match the dyes available to weavers in the 16th century.

The saloon looks accurate, even though red leather seems such a modern addition. It isn't: dyeing leather red predates the Druids. It's perfect for a hunting lodge.

RUSSELL STREET INN

Location: ORANGEBURG, SOUTH CAROLINA, USA
Interior Design: OLIVIA NEECE PLANNING & DESIGN
Architecture: DAVID SHAW
Photography: JONATHAN HILLYER

A 100-year-old American railroad hotel with falling plaster, mildew everywhere, and corroded plumbing. Small rooms with no closets. A candidate for the wrecker's ball, especially in America, where you could put up a new hotel almost overnight.

But instead, Olivia Neece and Susan Parham went to work under the auspices of the South Carolina Trust for Historical Preservation.

Old craftsmen were found to repair and reproduce plaster ornamentation. Whatever was salvageable was stripped and sanded of many colors. There were 26 paint colors in the building, from no specific source, so a local paint company matched them under the designer's eye. Missing and damaged mouldings were reproduced by a local millworker.

The nightmare became a dream, the Russell Street Hotel. The present designers found and salvaged quite a few American Queen Anne and Chippendale pieces, as well as several refined examples of Victorian style.

Its guest room design became a Gold Key finalist in 1986, and the lobby won the Designer's Circle first prize. All this on a tight budget in a small Southern town.

It's a town and a hotel with a can-do spirit, and the miracle of Russell Street was made possible by local artisans who had the skills (and love for their town) to bolster the designers' plans.

This toile is only one of four guest room schemes. The matching wood colors are complemented by soft blues, and accented by the gilt-colored mirror.

This stunning lobby with its restored columns, ceilings and floors is a tribute to the wedding of superior design with outstanding local craftsmanship.

Framed by restored pillars and replastered ceilings is this series of period chandeliers, with wall lighting to replicate the gas lights used in old railroad hotels.

PARK HOTEL
KENMARE

Location: KENMARE, COUNTY KERRY, IRELAND

At or beyond the brink of failure several times during its history, the Park Hotel Kenmare has been rejuvenated into a highly successful deluxe hotel.

Named 1988 Hotel of the Year for England and Ireland by the prestigious Egon Ronay Guide, as well as one of Fodor's Selected Hotels of Europe and a favorite of The Ackerman Guide, this deluxe Irish country house hotel provides an eclectic mix of classic and contemporary which creates a strong identity.

Its front foyer embodies the essence of Victorian charm. As befits a country house setting, this area is more living than registration area, with its cheery fireplace and velvet chairs. Its patterned carpet and circular chandelier frame important details such as period wall sconces and unique works of art.

Guest rooms run the gamut from Victorian to quasi-modern without interrupting the environment of this historic building. Because of its sophisticated, upscale clientele, the hotel's guest rooms feature amenities necessary for the 1980s: private bathrooms, radios, direct-dial telephones and individual heat controls.

It is the furnishings themselves that set the tone for the hotel's 50 guest rooms. Antique armoires and dressers, accented by mirrors, become pleasing focal points for design. Polished four-posters carry the eye upward in some rooms, while twin headboards, magnificently carved, vary the furniture heights in others.

In the public spaces, colors are rich and strong, for the most part, while in the guest rooms they are soothing and subdued. Small prints, used on wallcoverings and in carpets, make each area unique and interesting.

Bedroom suite and foyer are filled with antiques in solid Victorian style. The double headboards and footboards and the circular pattern in the foyer carpeting show an attention to detail that creates a style consistent with great design.

COUNTRY HOSPITALITY INN

Location:	BURNSVILLE, MINNESOTA, USA
Hotel Company:	RADISSON HOTEL CORP.
Interior Design:	CSA, INC.
Architecture:	BRW ARCHITECTS
Photography:	LEA BABCOCK

A prototype country inn at budget prices, whose guests enjoy the ambience, is Country Hospitality Inn, up in America's pine country of Minnesota.

"Creating residential appearance within hotel performance specifications" was the toughest part of the design. This is the part of the world with deep snow and cold, then long summer days, so maintaining a very natural look is a necessity.

There is a very heavy use of wood. Douglas fir, knotty pine, cedar and hardwood accents are the traditions in the northern USA.

Of specific interest are the wood floors in many public areas, wide planks recreating the sawmill generation as opposed to the thinner lathing used in later 20th century residential construction.

Complementing the hotel is the Country Kitchen Restaurant and Pub, located next door—this separation is becoming increasingly popular for limited service hotels. The designers worked within the framework of a $26,400 per room budget, which included everything except the cost of the land.

This 3-Star hotel was designed so that owners can add (or subtract) eight-room modules, and there are plans to build them throughout the world.

Even though this is the prototype for a chain, each unit will have the one-of-a-kind charm of a rustic country inn. Although prototype designs include stencilled borders and lace swags, each unit lends itself to the design ambience of its geographical location.

Wooden floors, lintels and beams are traditional and beautiful, and the designer found that tile around the fireplace is far superior to the usual red brick in this setting. Selecting the right area carpet completes the rustic environment.

Heavy on tradition with warm woods and floral accents, this room features intertwined country details such as grapevine wreaths over the bed and a brass headboard.

This china cabinet evokes the basic design of a peculiarly American piece of kitchen furniture: the Hoosier cabinet, in which the lower table top was covered with tin for rolling dough.

CURZON ON PARK LANE

Location: LONDON, ENGLAND
Hotel Company: HILTON INTERNATIONAL
Interior Design: TAVERN FURNISHING LTD.

A 5-star hotel on London's most prestigious thoroughfare is Curzon on Park Lane, a continental hotel with a long history.

Small and exclusive, the Curzon faced a problem unique to the high quality construction field: the repair, renovation and replacement of such materials as marble. The cutting and fitting of marble, and the matching of it, requires great skill—and the designer, in this case the TFL Group, couldn't cut any corners because of the demands of the clientele. This was a typically challenging task in the Curzon. The work was done floor by floor while other floors were in full occupancy.

Such small, old, elegant, 5-star hotels put pressure on designers, because of the exactness required in the selection of furniture (especially fabric). In many cases, extremely old patterns have to be found, along with mills to reproduce them.

Some built-in items of furniture remained after the renovation, but the 80 rooms and suites received a French style "boudoir" treatment which was carried through into the public areas.

The style is straight Louis XVI, as befits a continental hotel.

Fabrics had to be suited to Louis XVI furniture and bed valances, and drapery had to be matched throughout with wall coverings and lighting.

There is an upward flow of textures in this bedroom, as the long, thick spread moves up to the padded headrest and finally the airiness of the valances over the bed and above the window.

GRAYSTONE
GUEST HOUSE

Location: WILMINGTON, NORTH CAROLINA, USA
Interior Design: PERRY & PLUMMER DESIGN ASSOCIATES
Photography: J. BLOW

It took two years to convert the Bridgers mansion in Wilmington into the Graystone Guest House, even though it only has six guest rooms.

Each step was taken with the expertise of townsmen who formed the Wilmington Historical District. The massive building belies its outward appearance, because it is styled as a "small European-style inn."

In each of the widely varied rooms, breakfast is served on fine china with fine silver. The inspired restoration of the music room, drawing room, sitting room and dining room allows guests to experience the refinement of a bygone era.

Major systems replacement could

only be done without harming any of the elegant restoration, mostly in woodwork and plaster. But central air-conditioning and private baths were added, even though the overwhelming scope of the building makes it seem as if the structure is impregnable.

The six rooms, the St. James, de Rosset, Burgwin-Wright, Bridgers, Latimer and St. Thomas, feature different color schemes and bed frame types. All contain fireplaces, yet each is furnished in a different version of what a European Inn looked like in previous centuries. The St. James has royal purple draperies and semi-Victorian furniture; while the deRosset has its thin brass four-poster and French salon

chairs, and the modern-looking Burgwin-Wright includes almost Dutch clean lines and floral quilts.

The woodwork and plaster work in the drawing room and dining room are remarkable. The drawing room has especially unique Georgian pillars, intricately worked.

As in all historical districts, the Graystone is set amid restored shops and restaurants, which enhances its own sense of place.

Rewiring, central air-conditioning, and restoring this massive building had to be done without any destruction to the facade or interior walls.

In the St. Thomas room, the wooden four-poster and the antique furniture accent the restorative work on wood and plaster.

Bridgers Room in pinks and blues with thin wooden headboards give a feel of a French salon, a decorating scheme very popular in the American South during the 18th and 19th centuries.

THORNBURY CASTLE

Location: BRISTOL, ENGLAND

It's hard to keep your head about you when visitng Thornbury Castle, for it was once owned by Henry VIII, who stayed there with Ann Boleyn.

It's the only genuine castle in the south of England which operates as a hotel. It has 18 luxury bedrooms, some with huge four-posters and oriel windows overlooking the walled Tudor gardens. Its famous restaurant, one of the finest in England, has won an Egon Ronay "Restaurant of the Year" title.

It was built at the beginning of the 16th century by the third Duke of Buckingham, whose father was beheaded by Richard III. Then his executor, Henry VIII, kept the castle. Before she became queen, Mary Tudor lived there.

Two fine baronial dining rooms have paneled walls, heraldic shields and large open fireplaces, and the old dungeons are now cellars for fine wines.

In a magnificent setting in the West Country, close to Stratford-on-Avon, Thornbury Castle is a designer's dream.

Its traditional library features book-lined walls, an open fireplace, and an excellent oriel window.

Fabrics and furnishings in this castle/hotel match those discovered in historical accounts of Tudor interiors.

As in many other historic and historical hotels in this chapter, the arts of the architect and the interior designer are inextricably intertwined. Designers, particularly, consult museums to observe patterns and colorizations of fabrics no longer made.

Thornbury Castle is a tribute to the ability of the designer to recreate ancient richnesses.

Although the windows and fireplaces are the main architectural features, the generous fabric in the bed's canopy makes the four-poster the focal point of this outstanding example of baronial design.

VILLA
SAN MICHELE

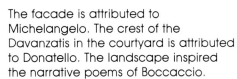

Location: FIRENZE (FLORENCE), ITALY
Architecture: GERARD GALLET

The facade is attributed to Michelangelo. The crest of the Davanzatis in the courtyard is attributed to Donatello. The landscape inspired the narrative poems of Boccaccio.

The setting is Florence, the house is the Villa Hotel San Michele. The 15th century Franciscan monastery is on a site venerated by the Etruscans, those little-known predecessors of the Romans.

In World War II, direct cannon hits gravely damaged it. In 1950 Lucien Teissier of Paris bought it and began restoration. Architects worked with the Florentine supervisors of historical monuments to repair the villa to original purity—and, to defray the expense, converted it to an awe-inspiring hotel. The Villa Hotel San Michele is historic Firenze.

Few reminders of its monastic past remain: except for the time worn, polished floors, the narrow-paned windows, and a front desk as austere as a monk's table. Designers introduced all of the touches necessary to create the look of humanistic luxury: sparkling crystal chandeliers, patterned area rugs with the light touch of an illuminated manuscript and beds crowned by canopies of fine fabric.

Overall, the interior design relies heavily on elegantly carved furnishings that reflect the graceful archways leading through this historic building. A color palette of ivory, touched with brights, completes this tasteful restoration.

The design of the lobby, formerly the chapel of the 15th century monastery, complements the flow of the arches with carpets that follow Oriental designs introduced to Italy during the Renaissance.

MARQUESA HOTEL

Location:	KEY WEST, FLORIDA, USA
Interior Design:	MACDONALD DESIGN GROUP
Architecture:	TOM POPE
Photography:	DAN FORER

The Marquesa Hotel is a 105-year-old building, an old five-dollar-a-night boarding house.

Now it's a small luxury hotel.

And it was the unanimous—and only—winner of the prestigious Master Craftsmanship Award of the Historic Florida Keys Preservation Board; the work took eight months.

This sparkling Victorian gem has marble baths and magnificent windows: "attention to detail in the reproduction of bay windows" was specifically noted by the excited Preservation Board judges. They also noted that to match existing woodwork, craftsmen had to create special cutting blades.

It is on the National Register of Historic Places, and was under strict guidelines from the National Park Service. The walls are pine tongue-and-groove. The duplication of existing details was the toughest part of the job: crown mouldings, architraves, and parts of interior staircases.

Once a fragile old boarding house, the Marquesa now has 15 magnificent rooms.

The design and the architecture must match exceedingly well in these official historic buildings. New electrics, sprinklers, and private baths were installed without any sacrifice to the historic integrity.

Rather than freezing the hotel in time, and recreating Victoriana, the Marquesa is meant to be true to its history—the fact that it has a past and a present.

Drawn from its boarding house past is the peek-a-boo kitchen, but its interior stairwells are perfect turn-of-the-century rehabilitations.

It cost $1.8 million for the 15 rooms, a substantial investment even with the significant tax credits available to historic sites.

This elegant interior stairwell is graced with an Italian-style carved wood table and gilt mirror.

Broken plaster effect in the dining room recreates boarding house history. It is as remarkable as the restored pillars and lintels. "MIRA" at the top refers to a new restaurant venture initiated by Marquesa's food specialists., Proal Perry and Norman van Aken.

PFLAUMS
POSTHOTEL

Location: PEGNITZ, WEST GERMANY
Interior Design: ROSENTHAL AG, CREATIV-TEAM/
                   HOTEL-DESIGN
Architecture: ROSENTHAL AG, CREATIV-TEAM/
                   HOTEL-DESIGN
Photography: OLAF JOCHBERG

When your guests are John Paul Getty, Daniel Barenboim, Henry Kissinger and the Aga Khan, you'd hope to win the Oscar from the Hotel Sales and Marketing Association! Which is just what happened to a surprised Dirk Obliers, Rosenthal's design chief, as the festival suites in the Pflaums Posthotel were named "Suites of the Year 2000."

Innovative, creative, surprising—shocking, perhaps? Yet, the rooms won instant acceptance from conservative guests, even though one has quadrophonic stereo in an endless star-studded sky over a bed, and another has a breakfast area integrated into the heating system.

Posthotel abandoned the norm and leaped to the far end of avant garde.

Often, the long, straight lines associated with Danish furniture have been converted to gentle arcs, and the chords of these arcs are not kept parallel to floors or walls. Gone is the traditional one-level horizontality which is so boring to the eye. There is a remarkable uni-color use of fabric in large statements, possible only when heights have been broken up in rooms with sufficient open areas.

Pflaums Posthotel's festival rooms escape uniformity, and do so without creating a new uniformity. They'll still be special in the year 2000.

Varied black and white triangular shapes on a gray background of the wall hanging contrast well with the deep red wall-to-wall carpeting in this contemporary bedroom.

Guests sleep under the stars with quadrophonic sound. The television is free-supported, and well above table level, for easy, yet avant-garde viewing.

The unconventional shape of this dark leather chair enhances the geometric configuration, while massive color patches in red and pink are energized by the vivid sofa fabric.

WEQUASETT INN
ON CAPE COD

Location: PLEASANT BAY, CHATHAM,
                    MASSACHUSETTS, USA
Interior Design: GRUWELL-PHEASANT DESIGN
Architecture: WILLIAM TABLER & ASSOCIATES
Photography: RUSSELL ABRAHAM

Wequasett Inn on Cape Cod is a
waterfront/beach resort of 18 separate
buildings, which include historical 18th
century structures such as the Eben
Ryder House and the Jensen Nickerson
House (which dates to 1740).

The designer created schemes for 36
new rooms and remodeled 20 existing
units. But this is a fresh interpretation of a
Cape Cod bed and breakfast inn.

The new rooms were split into five
separate color schemes to reinforce a
more residential ambience. Bright,
vibrant colors were used not normally
associated with Cape Cod.

A wide variety of very un-Cape Cod
accessories were added: ''readable''
books for clients' use, silk flowers in
unique baskets, Amari bowls and hand-
painted wooden toys.

The designer's objective was to give
a residential feeling to a growing resort.
Because of the large number of
separate buildings, guests have a
choice of environments. With a
secondary market of conferences that
attract guests who don't necessarily
come for the traditional seaside
vacations, the designer is able to move
away from strict tradition.

*Fabric color and texture
played up by quilts and
upholsterings, become the
focal points of these
unconventional, colorful Cape
Cod rooms.*

FAIRMOUNT HOTEL

Location:	SAN ANTONIO, TEXAS, USA
Interior Design:	DESIGN CONTINUUM
Architecture:	ALAMO ARCHITECTS
Photography:	IRA MONTGOMERY

Vacant and run-down, the Fairmount Hotel was slated for destruction in 1980 when the San Antonio Preservation Society saved it from being torn down.

The city leased a vacant site six blocks away, and the hotel was moved to it. It had 37 rooms and weighed 16,000 tons.

But there was some luck. The building, built in 1906, had never been tampered with. So the original was where you could see it, renovate it, and work with it. A new addition of 10 more rooms was built, in the same Italianate style as the original.

Traditional red brick and yellow adobe were used in the new wing. Once it weathers, it will look like the old.

The overall interior design is true to turn-of-the-century, with stone lamps and bleached wood floors. No two guest rooms are alike—there are high ceilings, great expanses of window, and most rooms have balconies.

Furnishings are indigenous to the Southwest: marble floors from Mexico, Indian motif throw rugs, and similar items.

Most of the colors are desert colors: sunset peaches and sand beige. The rooms have very high ceilings and large windows, requiring delicate fabrics.

The interiors are so fine they won first place in the hospitality category of the American Society of Interior Designers.

This suite magnificently emphasizes both the high ceilings and natural light that pours in. Just as different heights of the doorways in the passage are counterpointed by the four-poster, so the oval chair back mirrors the oval tabletop.

This original third floor hallway,
with a skylight added to it,
draws on the traditional
Southwestern use of brick in
interior walls.

CHAPTER 3

Business Hotels

Robert DiLeonardo

*B*usiness hotels didn't always begin as business hotels, or even hotels that attracted a business-oriented clientele.

Over the past two decades, some properties became business hotels for a variety of reasons: they were in downtown centers of cities with booming commerce and trade, they were resorts suddenly popular for business meetings or conventions, or they were traditional hotels that happened to start life with the good fortune of having available space to convert to conference centers.

Other hotels were specifically built for the business market, even planned around the need for convenient audio-visual presentations, private luncheons, and conventions. Still other hotels had none of this, but went out and created it because the tremendous surge of business travel made it a market too good to overlook.

Robert DiLeonardo of DiLeonardo International, Inc., hotel and restaurant designers from Warwick, Rhode Island, USA, gives it this definition: "A business hotel caters to the special needs of the working professional who is traveling for business reasons."

He contrasts them with other hotels in this fashion: "The marketing edge leans toward efficiency, service and speed, rather than comfort and relaxation." He warns that a successful business hotel should, in addition to fast check-in and express check-out, ". . . have all the conveniences of a modern office." These requirements have changed the design mandate for hotels.

"Room designs and furnishings must be business sensitive . . . a larger desk with good lighting is needed, because the business traveler must often convert his room into an office." Looking into the future, he sees new technology: viewing phones and personal fax machines in the rooms.

"Enhance the purpose of the space!" DiLeonardo advises. "It benefits the hotel to create board room spaces that are conducive to decision-making . . . that is, a feeling of importance is created for the occupants."

"To prevent redundancy, regional influences, whether architectural or cultural, should be incorporated into the design. Trendy designs become outdated," says DiLeonardo.

HOLIDAY INN

Location: NEW LONDON, CONNECTICUT, USA
Hotel Company: HOLIDAY CORP.
Interior Design: HOTEL SERVICES DIVISION OF
HOLIDAY CORP.
Architecture: LYMAN GOFF ARCHITECT

An unusual theme for a business hotel, "intimate European lodging," was selected for the Holiday Inn, New London, Connecticut, USA.

Because this urban roadside motel's clientele includes both business people and families, the intimate theme encourages the commercial traveler to return, accompanied by family.

This Holiday Inn has 135 rooms, along with an atrium, restaurant, lounge, meeting and board rooms. The long, narrow atrium is stunning with its reverse curves of flying buttresses atop classical greek columns. The columns are doubled, counterpointing the twin natural lights from above: skylighting along the chord, and a glass "wall" from the top of the arch down to the true roof.

Huge dark leather chairs, separated by marble-topped tables, create a perfect geometry in the blue and white lobby. Extensive use is made of cane-type tropical foliage, with accents of fresh flowers.

This hotel is an oasis of quiet under-statement in the bustling, industrial Northeastern USA, but that understate-ment is made in large tones in large public spaces: the focal point of the atrium, for example, is the atrium itself. The interior design is the architecture. By contrast, in the lobby, the architecture is kept simple to emphasize the enveloping chairs.

The business guest should enjoy these big, bold strokes.

A blue-and-white muted motif downplays the desk and focuses on large, magnificent chairs in the lobby.

The atrium is the message.
This inspiring and classic bold
design is its own focal point.

RADISSON
PLAZA VII

Location: MINNEAPOLIS, MINNESOTA, USA
Hotel Company: RADISSON HOTEL CORP.
Interior Design: CSA, INC.
Architecture: WZMH GROUP INC./
HAMMELL GREEN, ABRAHAMSON
Photography: LEA BABCOCK

The original Radisson was built in Minneapolis in 1909, but in 1984 it was imploded to build a 363-room Radisson Plaza VII hotel as part of a mixed-use facility that includes upscale retail shopping and extensive office space.

The target market was the upper income, executive traveler. Public spaces are dramatic, with a 17-story atrium at their core.

The lobby was designed to create an awesome sense of arrival. There is a lavish use of fine finishing materials, such as marble and rich millwork. There is a 3,000-pound marble sphere in constant motion, revolving from pressure created by a water pump beneath.

Guest rooms and suites are water marks of comfort, as befits the site of the original Radisson. They feature large desks, and high-quality, residential furnishings. Bathrooms are uniquely designed to emphasize spaciousness, and display an extensive use of marble.

But the many suites are not to be taken in common. They are eclectic and international, using furnishings from many periods and many parts of the world. The board rooms are so popular they demand lengthy advance notice for meetings. One features a reddish motif akin to the common perception of an old British private club, but it has a square table designed with flattened corners so that everyone has full vision.

These design touches address the problems of sophisticated businessmen, without sacrificing any of the interior design.

As Radisson's flagship, the hotel displays a leading edge of design that points toward what the chain will do in the future.

By flattening corners, this square conference table gives clear sightlines from every position.

Pink and rose, with gold metal accents, enhanced with the generous use of glass, leave a clean line unusual for such a large room.

In this suite, overstuffed pink furniture and carpet, with gold accessories, repeat the theme from bar (above).

RAMADA
RENAISSANCE
HAMBURG

Location: HAMBURG, WEST GERMANY
Hotel Company: RAMADA, INC.
Interior Design: KAAF GMBH
Architecture: VON GERKAN-MARG & PARTNER
Photography: CREATIVE SOURCES

Hamburg is one of the most famous historical towns of Europe: although a large city, many still call it a "town" because of its ancient history.

The Ramada Renaissance Hamburg is part of that history, with its massive, magnificent walls. Its facade is classified as a historical monument, and the building was once the printery of the oldest newspaper in Hamburg.

With 211 guest rooms and suites, five function rooms and a health club, the interior designer decided that "very traditional" was the only answer. Thus the inspiration for the interiors is Hanseatic, dating to the days of the Hanseatic league, when German work-manship was heavily traded on the waterways of Europe.

The rooms have extra large beds, eiderdown quilts, and pure cotton bed linens. There is a unique Renaissance suite of 1,800 square feet, with a large living room, two bedrooms, three baths, a kitchen and a bar. All guests have use of the sauna, pool, solarium and whirlpool.

The lobby has a circular "slot" check-in desk such as those specially built for northern European hotels of the early 19th century. A magnificent sea horse catches the eye of every first-time visitor.

The hotel is part of the Hanse-Viertel, Europe's longest shopping arcade.

When asked about the problems faced in fashioning a property that is part monument, part mall, and part of the ancient downtown, the designer unhesitatingly replied, "none!"

That's hard to believe, considering that in addition to all of the above, the designer made a showpiece of the Noblesse restaurant, one of the finest hotel restaurants in Europe.

Fascinating desk and wooden columns are lightened with white curtains and light marble tables and grey upholstered chairs. Desk shape repeated in white above is stunning.

WHITE SWAN HOTEL

Location: GUANGZHO, CHINA
Interior Design: HIRSCH/BEDNER & ASSOCIATES
Architecture: C.N. SHEH

Hordes of business people trooping through a business hotel is a manager's dream. But the White Swan, in Guangzho—old Canton—China, has a problem of foot traffic that is a source of pride for a designer.

Non-guests, and non-businessmen, tromp through in amazing numbers just to look at this 1,000-room hotel, with architecture by no less a personage than the vice-president of China's architectural society, C.N. Sheh, and design by Hirsch/Bedner.

The White Swan was the first of the posh, Western-style hotels to open in China. A glance at the lobby shows why both travelers and native Chinese are so fascinated by it: red pillars and interior pagoda-style roofs hold up large Western balconies topped with delicate asparagus ferns. Multi-leveled octagonally-shaped walkways wend their way through the immense greenery of South China shrubbery.

There is an atrium effect with a waterfall, but instead of the curved lines usually associated with atrium design, the ceiling is a large, flat skylight, framed again by the red pillars, long white balconies, and tropical plants.

Suites are magnificent, continuing this blend of Western and Chinese. Gold and crystal chandeliers of the French style are complemented by Gaullic wrought-iron framed doorways. Wall screens are Chinese in wood or painted enamel. The eclectic furniture—some of it thickly upholstered—is most often associated with American hotels.

Although opened in 1983, it is already a legend in China. It marries Chinese and Western styles—as much in the guest rooms as in the public spaces —and is a text for interested students, which is why this luxury business hotel has so many. China may soon begin the export of many of its own designers and architects, whose native techniques have often been copied in foreign hotels.

Blend of Western and Chinese design in Presidential suite masterfully creates both a feeling of comfort and a sense of place.

A flat skylight supported by pagoda-like pillars surrounds the waterfall in this cross-cultural atrium.

RAMADA RENAISSANCE ALEXANDRIA

Location: ALEXANDRIA, EGYPT
Hotel Company: RAMADA , INC.
Architecture: INTERNATIONAL DESIGN &
                     FURNISHING LTD./
                     CAIRO INVESTMENT &
                     DEVELOPMENT COMPANY
Photography: CREATIVE SOURCES

Designing a business hotel in Alexandria, Egypt, is just a bit more exciting than most places, for Alexandria was once the intellectual capital of the world. Some 2,000 years ago, an architect or a designer could learn his craft from the city's fabled library, the repository of unique educational scrolls found nowhere else.

Alexandria is a city of large ideas, Egypt's ancient gateway to the rest of the world. The Ramada Renaissance Alexandria is a tall, bold building overlooking the Mediterranean Sea, shaped hexagonally with balconies on almost every room. It looks a bit like those war

engines used to scale the walls of ancient cities.

In the lobby, a magnificent planter sets an octagonal theme, surrounded by four sofa areas with octagonal tables. These tables are blonde wood framed with dark woods to match the check-in desk. Gold chandeliers are inset with purple and white glass to match the upholstering.

Just as the sifting sands of Egypt create a natural spaciousness around the infrequent oases, so the designer's decision not to add additional chairs creates a natural spaciousness around the sofas.

Yet as broadly stated as this hotel had to have been, it must first serve the businessman as skillfully as the scribes of the Library of Alexandria once served the guests of the world.

Each room is individually air-conditioned, an important touch along the Mediterranean where guests from many lands differ in what they consider too hot or too cold. There are 200 rooms, including some with more than just a bedroom, and suites. The combination of Mediterranean and more traditional hotel designs is in character with Alexandria's cosmopolitan history.

Rich purples identify this lobby's theme as Mediterranean, complemented by the designer's octagonal plan for conversation areas.

RADISSON PLAZA
AT TOWN CENTER

Location: SOUTHFIELD, MICHIGAN, USA
Hotel Company: RADISSON HOTEL CORP.
Interior Design: CSA, INC.
Architecture: SIKES JENNINGS, KELLY
Photography: GEORGE HEINRICH

The Radisson Plaza at Town Center in Southfield, Michigan, USA, is targeted to the upscale commercial business traveler. The city is part of Detroit's extended automotive empire, so "ordinary design" is out of the question.

Since the architect chose to make big architectural statements, the designer was working with a structure of many hard surface materials. The decision? To soften and humanize the space, using a contemporary look with rich finish materials such as wood and stone.

In most key areas, the colorization is in mauve, burgundy and jade green, with guest rooms echoing this public space palette.

Exhaustive, frequent meetings with the owner, operator contractor, architect, and designer, made it possible for such a bold design to succeed.

There are some minimalist treatments in public areas, where the designer wants the statements to be made by the architect, but a reverse trend in other areas—including guest rooms—where intimacy and privacy are required, and the architect is the backdrop for the designer.

Some restaurant areas look as if the architect specifically built to enhance the designer's ideas. There is a private dining room where muted pink and light burgundy are the entirety of the place settings and chair fabrics, while the walls are of rich-looking, dark woods. These woods are repeated in the chair arms, showing a high level of cooperation between architect and designer.

This mauve and burgundy setting, with its extensive use of glass, perfectly complements the wooden columns and mouldings.

Minimalist lobby design features just a few floral brass planters and framing plants. It emphasizes the columned architecture with its graceful stairway.

Although three meals a day are served here, the jade green and burgundy setting looks intimate. Brass rails and plants break up the spaces. The architecture complements the design.

RAMADA
RENAISSANCE
KARLSRUHE

Location: KARLSRUHE, WEST GERMANY
Hotel Company: RAMADA, INC.
Interior Design: HILTON DESIGN STUDIO
Architecture: PROF. RIEDL
Photography: CREATIVE SOURCES

The Ramada Renaissance Karlsruhe, centrally located in an historic, lovely city, is designed with several styles: one restaurant is stunningly early Victorian, while another is "rustical" and specializes in regional dishes.

It's an appropriate combination, because the Karlsruhe is near the famous palace Markgraf von Baden, whose early Victorian architecture and furnishings are a tourist's delight.

With a primary market of commercial business travelers in its 207 rooms, it offers eight conference and meeting rooms, accommodating from 6 to 80 people. The grand ballroom holds 300.

With some very notable exceptions, the design is modern, counterpointed by the Victorian and rustic. The lobby is in plain woods with straight-line, upholstered furniture. The yellowed ceiling lighting provides a softening effect reminiscent of the gaslights formerly used in European hotel lobbies.

But the ceiling also is mirrored and beamed, emphasizing the richness of unadorned woods. The painting over the check-in desk owes its ancestry to the Cubists, and is delightfully reflected by the ceiling mirrors.

The modern design is unexpected inside a structure built of such German traditional red brick. Inside, many public areas repeat another traditional German design element: beamed ceilings.

The interior design is very modern for traditional Karlsruhe; elsewhere, it might be called contemporary.

A stunning bar area continues the theme of light woods reaching up to dark wood beams, with a lateral complement of the foreground carpet whose colors are reflected in seating area at rear.

Simplicity in wood and glass can create a subtle architecture. Dining chairs in pinks and greens, coordinate with the table setting to complete the environment.

MÖVENPICK/
RADISSON

Location: LAUSANNE, SWITZERLAND
Hotel Company: MÖVENPICK HOTELS/RADISSON HOTEL CORP.
Interior Design: MÖVENPICK PROJECTS, AG
Architecture: SUTER & SUTER
Photography: YVES RYNCKI

With all the natural beauties of Switzerland, a business hotel must do more than simply open its doors. The Mövenpick/Radisson in Lausanne has a modern design very much in keeping with the country's Alpine reputation: extensive open spaces.

Few hotels have such a wide variety of lighting. There are stage spotlights in some areas, and wildly unique chandeliers in others: one is green, with plain, ball-shaped lights in a circular form over wooden tables set in red and white, while another is a massive brass menagerie ending in delicate tulip-cup shades with serrated edges.

There's a bar area that mixes red leather seat backs and cane chairs with brilliantly-colored circular mobiles in which the Italianate reds, greens and yellows predominate. The wooden ceiling is dotted with lights, separated by avant-garde shapes that look as if they are painted on glass.

A dining room is then done quietly in green and chrome, made intimate by flowering trees.

The public areas are so spacious that occasional glass and chrome pillars are needed to give perspective. But every-where, there is an unusual theme: the heavy use of design on ceilings to give each room its own, powerfully unique character.

With 265 rooms, the Mövenpick has plenty of businessmen stretching their necks to look at its ceilings, but looking down completes the picture: in some places carpeting is neutral to maintain intimacy, in other places it is incredibly plush and colorful, and still elsewhere the excitement is provided by the traditional wooden floors of a Swiss chalet.

Leather, cane, wood and mobiles—a rich treatment somewhere between avant-garde and trendy, but in any case absolutely unique.

Very traditional dining in intimate greens and yellows, lighted from unusual chandeliers, is just one of many different design ideas used in the Mövenpick.

OMNI HOTEL AT CHARLESTON PLACE

Location:	CHARLESTON, SOUTH CAROLINA, USA
Hotel Company:	OMNI HOTELS CORPORATION
Interior Design:	WILSON & ASSOCIATES
Photography:	ROBERT MILLER

From the mahogany panels of the Shaftesbury Room, through the glass roof and louvred shutters of the Palmetto Cafe, to the high-energy Water Colors lounge, the Omni Charleston Place Hotel looks just like what it is: a business hotel with a tremendous emphasis on design.

The lobby has a sweeping grand staircase leading to the ballroom, accented by a 12-foot chandelier custom made in Venice. It is filled with antiques from Sotheby's. "No expense was spared to create this intrinsically Southern scene with its selection of English furniture and painted paneling detail, with a palette of celadon, salmon and burgundy," says Trisha Wilson, the US-based designer.

The "Old South" theme isn't just for public areas. The guest rooms themselves follow the theme, and each is unique—both in design and layout. Some even have balconies overlooking downtown Charleston.

Red and green floral prints—very bold—dominate guest room design. Custom-designed case pieces incorporate the traditional Georgian lines with simple elegance. The mini-bar is even hidden in the armoire.

Each room even has a ceiling fan, which means 475 of them, because the Omni looms large in the middle of Charleston's historical district.

Everywhere in public areas are iron and brass hand railings.

Elegant, typically Southern columns with traditional crown moldings lend even more elegance.

The green, gold and black Shaftesbury restaurant was built for yet another reason: to be a plush restaurant for Charlestonians themselves, making the Omni a hotel where a business guest is very appreciated by his local clients when he invites them to "his place" for dinner.

Brass and wrought iron blend perfectly with native vegetation, as the open woodwork in the roof adds perspective to the semi-formality of this area.

Elegant chandeliers and a lovely green marble table counterpoint the mahogany walls in this intimate, high-ceilinged bar area.

THE HILTON HOTEL, OCALA

Location: OCALA, FLORIDA, USA
Hotel Company: HILTON HOTELS CORP.
Interior Design: LYNN WILSON ASSOCIATES
Architecture: DEEDER, RICHEY & SIPLE
Photography: FRANCETIC PHOTO ASSOCIATES, INC.

Not all business is conducted in the skycrapers of urban canyons, and not all business hotels are cut from the same gray flannel decor.

Lynn Wilson Associates' designers exploded the myths of cookie-cutter business hotel design when they fashioned the interiors for the Hilton Hotel in Ocala, Florida.

Lynn Wilson felt strongly that the hotel's spaces should emphasize, not downplay, its geographic setting. "Our concept was to design a hotel environment that would suitably reflect a Florida atmosphere yet recognize the traditional local character of Ocala, a city whose major revenue comes from world class horse breeders," explained Wilson.

Her solution was to use pastels or neutrals on large, architectural elements to keep the spaces open and airy—even during hot summer days. She selected upholstery and drapery materials, as well as accent rugs, in botanical prints to bring the lushness of Florida indoors. However, she avoided hot, tropical prints which would have destroyed the traditional theme of this 160-room property.

Ceiling heights used in modern construction pose one of the major challenges for designers. As in many newer hotels, innovative design is required to make spaces look higher and more impressive.

"Beams were installed at varied levels to give the illusion of greater height. We wanted all of the public space ceilings to make a strong visual statement and help move people through the areas," Wilson added.

By creating a step-down "sunken" living room and expanding the vertical impact of the bed with a floor-to-ceiling draped pavilion, no walls were necessary to define the separate areas of the Hilton's Presidential Suite.

HYATT ON COLLINS

Location:	MELBOURNE, AUSTRALIA
Hotel Company:	HYATT INTERNATIONAL CORP.
Interior Design:	HIRSCH/BEDNER & ASSOCIATES
Architecture:	PEDDLE, THORP & LEARMONTH
Photography:	JAIME ARDILES-ARCE

In many respects, the Hyatt on Collins is Australia in microcosm: a dynamic blending of old and new in a setting made stunning by natural beauty.

This 580-room hotel has the broad sweeping spaces appropriate for such an energetic and open continent. The atrium lobby, which climbs 71 feet, is not static space, but encompasses three levels of shopping and dining facilities.

The dining areas of the Hyatt on Collins had to be sophisticated enough to attract the international business travelers who make up much of the hotel's clientele as well as the cosmopolitan residents of Melbourne. Hirsch/Bedner relied on natural materials for maximum impact.

Framing the entrance to Max's, the hotel's specialty seafood restaurant, is a marble-lined foyer—just a small part of the 250,000 square feet valued at US$1.7 million used in the hotel. The designers complemented the gleaming black marble with a solid black granite floor, but established a strong contrast with brass accents.

Nature provides the central theme for the Plane Tree Cafe. Delicate trees are interspersed among tables to divide the room into small, private areas. Black lacquer-framed chairs, upholstered in beige, and marble-topped tables, void of any tablecloths, underscore this natural theme.

Marble is a motif for the Hyatt Collins, whether as a dramatic art element, as in the hotel's specialty dining area (left) or an architectural element, as in the floors and fountain base of the hotel's 71 foot high atrium.

Dramatically lighted and elegantly accented, a simple buffet becomes an effective design element.

A black granite floor shot with a cast brass crevasse gives diners an aesthetic taste of the sophistication they can expect from Max's restaurant.

SHERATON TARA HOTEL

Location: PARSIPPANY, NEW JERSEY, USA
Hotel Company: SHERATON CORP./TARA HOTELS
Interior Design: DILEONARDO INTERNATIONAL INC.

With its turreted facade and Tudor interiors, the Sheraton Tara transforms the "business hotel" into a corporate castle.

To achieve this effect in a modern, 389-room hotel, designers integrated contemporary and period-style pieces. Spatial relationships were particularly important. Strong architectural forms were highlighted to recreate the feeling of grand interior spaces associated with Tudor manors.

Designers with DiLeonardo International deliberately selected wall and floor treatments that would provide a correct Tudor-style frame for the furnishings. Multi-colored and intricately patterned stone floors in the public spaces flow upward into carved wood paneling and gothic plaster-applied relief work. A rough-hewn beamed ceiling establishes this theme in the lobby. Tapestry-covered, "throne chairs" and a central roundabout seating unit provide a softening counterpart to the sturdy overhead detail.

"We kept the public space corridors simple. But they do extend the design. We used a high travertine base and a red marble dado placed above head height, along with a warm gray matrix paint, to obtain a stone-like quality on the wall surface," explained Robert DiLeonardo.

Travertine was used again as the wainscotting in the Great Room. Anchored by a massive fireplace and a reflecting pool, this grand space is warmed by firelight colors: golden oak and ash in the woods, rich brocades and golden tans, as well as cameo-colored velvets used to cover the over-scaled lounge and sofa seating.

Warm woods and candlelight colors bring the "corporate castle" theme into the conference room. High-backed chairs circling the conference table lend design impact as well as a note of residential comfort.

DURHAM HILTON

Location: DURHAM, NORTH CAROLINA, USA
Hotel Company: HILTON HOTELS CORP.
Interior Design: ONE DESIGN CENTER
Architecture: ENVIRONTEK
Photography: WHITNEY COX

The demands of a hotel's target market determine not only the facilities and amenities required for the property; they also help establish the parameters for design.

"We had to create interiors that would appeal to both commercial travelers and the local university clientele," said Cyndi Folds, of One Design Center, based in Greensboro, North Carolina. Her solution for the 154-room Durham Hilton was to fashion a sleek and contemporary residential look that would be appreciated by either group of guests. However, to make the "modern" style more challenging, she dramatized both public spaces and guest rooms with judicious touches of Oriental accents.

Since both contemporary and Oriental design stress uncluttered, horizontal lines, the designers emphasized mid-rise room dividers and low, plush seating that would give the public spaces and restaurants a calm, open look. Except for wooded columns and artwork, this line carries through to the restaurant. Chairs and booths, framed in wood and upholstered in subtle stripes, flow around one restaurant in a fluid line, punctuated by plants. In another dining area, tables are screened by tasteful dividers capped with wood and brass.

Contrasting with this understated but elegant look is the high-energy design of the hotel's lounge. A dynamic overbar recreates the skyline of New York City in outlines of vibrantly patriotic red, white and blue neons. Smooth, reflective surfaces and rubberized tile provide a high-tech image and easy maintenance.

The bright lights of the "big city," New York, become the neon focus of this high-energy lounge. Soffits and awnings define the perimeter seating areas, while custom drink pods with mahogany trim encourage interaction from bar to dance floor.

INTERNATIONAL CROSSROADS SHERATON

Location: MAHWAH, NEW JERSEY, USA
Hotel Company: SHERATON CORP.
PRIME MOTOR INNS
Interior Design: INTERIOR DESIGN FORCE INC.
Architecture: THE GILCHRIST PARTNERSHIP
Photography: PETER PAIGE

The bold, geometric effect of the architecture's precise angles is multiplied by the clean lines of contemporary interior designed for the International Crossroads Sheraton.

"Our design plays off the 30- and 60-degree angles in the atrium lobby. But, we introduced elements with curves and circles to soften the look," noted Stephen D. Thompson, president of Interior Design Force based in New York City.

With the granite and glass framework of the building as a backdrop, the designers introduced curving sofas in deep blue and geometrically patterned accent rugs in cool gray and a warmer mauve. Wide spacing was necessary between the lobby seating areas because the space serves both the hotel and office center incorporated into this multi-use structure.

"We wanted the color and styles used in the lobby to continue through-out the hotel. However, it was important that each area be able to stand on its own aesthetically because the hotel's restaurant and function rooms attract both guests and local, suburban patrons," Thompson added.

For the nightclub, that thematic continuation sparked a new take on Art Deco, complete with checkerboard black-and-white tiled floor and wall accents. Even the blue accent color reappears—but in a slightly brighter value.

Geometric simplicity shapes the architecture and interior design in this lobby. The curving lines and deep blue used for the sofas soften the steep angles without inter-rupting the space's sleek profile.

A new take on Art Deco enlivens this lounge, while carrying through the geometric theme established in the hotel's lobby.

Bands of colorful tile contrasting with pristine white are the only accents needed in this space dominated by broad blue splashes of sky and water.

BOULEVARD
HOTEL
SINGAPORE

Location: SINGAPORE
Interior Design: DORA GAD LTD.
Architecture: R.S.P. ARCHITECTS/
                    DORA GAD LTD.
Photography: BERNARD KOH

Gone are the days when design and decorating were synonymous. Now, interior designers are not only aesthetic guides but true space planners.

Spatial considerations strongly influenced the interior design of Singapore's 375-room Boulevard Hotel.

"We took on this job because we were intrigued by the odd and difficult shapes of the interiors—especially the semicircular atrium which is only 18 feet wide but up to 15 floors high," commented designer Gad, head-quartered in Tel Aviv, Israel.

Her response to this challenge was to offset this strong circular motion with accents in sharp, diagonal lines both behind and on the front of the reception counter. She added a relief of cast aluminum to add visual interest and arrest the eye at points along the semicircular elevator core. However, two semicircular niches were installed so as not to eradicate any connection with the circularity.

Placement of a forest of structural columns also required close attention. The designers opted to envelop these columns in gold-tinted mirrors both to create a warmer look and visually widen the lobby space.

According to Gad, the mirrored columns also linked the look of the elevator core and lobby. "The aluminum relief reflects in the mirrored surfaces of the columns and tables. It also sparkles and creates interest for viewers on the ground floor or the 15 floors encircling the lobby."

The linearity and gold tones used for the hotel's lobby are translated into the executive suite. However, the textures and materials shift from cold-surfaced metals and mirrors to more residential polished woods and leathers.

HYATT REGENCY
TECH CENTER

Location: DENVER, COLORADO, USA
Hotel Company: HYATT HOTELS CORP.
Interior Design: WILSON & ASSOCIATES
Architecture: WZMH GROUP, INC.
Design Architecture: GELICK FORAN ASSOCIATES LTD.
Photography: ROBERT MILLER

High tech may offer an exciting business environment, but high touch is more inviting in business hotels.

That conclusion provided the theme for the interiors of the 450-room, US$60 million Hyatt Regency Tech Center hotel. A 12-story atrium links the hotel with a 15-story office building. Designers with Dallas-based Wilson & Associates used this space as an aesthetic link, as well. This lobby reflects a marriage of high tech and high touch. Metallic arches, made to look like cast iron, appropriately suggest Colorado's railroad center past, as well as its

technologically-oriented present. Grids of metallic arches span imposing, free-standing columns to recreate the feeling of a posh railway station.

Three guest room wings flow from this central core. Their design underscores their separation from the bustle of the lobby. While the public spaces are glittering and bold, guest rooms are natural and fresh. Most of the palettes borrow from western spring pastels—taupes, peaches and greens. And, unlike the lobby which recalls the iron and steel vigor of Colorado's pioneering past, the guest rooms reflect

its traditional arts and crafts. Generally, casegoods are knotted pine—not the rustic version suitable for cabins, but a gray-washed, more refined version.

Suites span a variety of styles from the spare elegance of Santa Fe to the welcoming jewel-toned pattern-on-pattern mix of historic ski resorts.

A residentially-styled fireplace plays up the warm, relaxed ambience of this suite, but also doubles as a room divider which separates living and working space.

The wrought-iron look of these dramatically illuminated barrel arches is mirrored by the black lacquer finish on the chairs and the architectural detail in the doorway.

This stunning circular table repeats the circular curves of the ends of the handrails used for the staircase that leads guests away from the registration area.

MAURYA
SHERATON

Location: NEW DELHI, INDIA
Hotel Company: SHERATON CORP./WELCOMGROUP
Interior Design: KIRAN PATKI
Architecture: RAJINDER KUMAR; SPACE CONSULTANTS
Photography: HARDEV SINGH

Just 10 minutes drive from New Delhi's airport or the bustling city center, the Maurya Sheraton offers the latest in facilities and services required by modern business travelers. But the interior design is an opulent remembrance of its country's past.

Every aspect of this 500-room property's design recalls the Mauryan era—India's first dynasty. The mood is set in the lobby, where wood and stone flow upwards gracefully to recreate a "chaitya" or Buddhist hall of worship. Between the wooden beams appear panels of a colorful mural by acclaimed artists M.F. Husain and Krishen Khanna. These paintings decorate the lobby ceiling with stylized scenes depicting people involved in activities from the mundane to the extraordinary.

The style of this mural is repeated in smaller panels capping the windows that frame the lobby.

Famous figures from the Mauryan era provide the design inspiration for each of the three presidential suites and 10 luxury suites. Inspired by the Chinese chronicler of the Mauryan empire, Fa-Hien, the suite bearing his name features elegant silk panels and delicate, hand-painted screens. It is illuminated by Chinese-style lamps and accented with accessories in burnished copper. Named after the famous Sufi poet, Firdausi, another suite reflects the splendor of ancient Persia—from its cool marble floors accented by Persian rugs, to the jewel tones of its upholstery fabric.

Though the Kamal Mahal ballroom reflects the Mauryan culture in less detail, it retains the spirit of this dynasty with bright, sunburst border trim framing the carpeting and glistening, shell-like chandeliers.

The intricate and richly patterned tapestry is an unexpected accent alongside the rustic table. However, the two are unified visually by the hot stripes of the banquette.

From the ceiling moldings to the chair frames and the carpet pattern, the spirit of the Mauryan dynasty pervades this room in the Maurya Sheraton, one of Sheraton's 1987 hotels of the year.

BEVERLY HERITAGE
HOTEL

Location: COSTA MESA, CALIFORNIA, USA
Interior Design: DILEONARDO INTERNATIONAL, INC.
Photography: MILROY/MCALEER

Today's business hotels must be an office away from the office and a home away from home. These requirements sparked a functionally efficient but residentially luxurious design concept for the Beverly Heritage Hotel.

Essential changes were made in the 238 guest rooms. These are rooms designed to be flexible enough for comfortable working or sleeping. Over-sized desks provide ample work room and are equipped with an outlet for a personal computer—either the guest's own or a complimentary portable personal computer available from the hotel.

Both in the guest rooms and public spaces colors are deep. "We used a dark emerald green and a tea rose pink as the corporate colors for this property," said Robert DiLeonardo, the Warwick, Rhode Island-based designer. "These colors with floral fabric accents are in strategic pieces in the lobby, in particular, to give guests the feeling of a weekend retreat."

The lobby/lounge area is flexible, as is the design. Plush upholstered lounge chairs and nouveau French arm chairs are meant to be moved—pulled up to function in groups not static design elements. This adaptability is especially important since the space is used throughout the day, from breakfast to

afternoon tea and evening cocktails.

Though the materials are rich in color, more casual accents keep the area from being too formal. Large-scale louvered shutters, in a pickled-wood finish sheath, and angled window walls form a casual and attractive backdrop. An intimate bar on the upper level doubles as a breakfast buffet.

The gleam of a highly-polished table top provides a visually interesting work surface for meetings. Simple artwork and cool walls underscore a light and airy look essential for long hours spent in high-powered meetings.

Though elegant in design, this room is also a workspace. The stylish desk provides ample room for papers and a telephone, and is properly lighted.

What better way to relax after a long, hard business day than in front of this sumptuous verde marble-framed fireplace, accented by the hotel's "corporate" colors: emerald green and tea rose pink.

COMPRI CUMBERLAND CENTER

Location: ATLANTA, GEORGIA, USA
Hotel Company: COMPRI HOTELS
Interior Design: INDEX THE DESIGN FIRM
Architecture: WHATLEY & PARTNERS

"Limited service" operations does not limit the design impact of the (Compri) Cumberland Center.

This new generation of business hotel eliminates the large, segmented public spaces. Instead, it combines the lobby, lounge, dining and meeting functions in one area—the Compri Club.

With no walls to subdivide these spaces, the Index's designers turned to design elements to set visual parameters for each area. Dark mahogany millwork and green marble were used to identify circulation areas. Comfortable, overstuffed seating, enriched with one-of-a-kind antiques, is arranged away from the traffic flow to provide an intimate setting for conversation.

Wooden shutters screen off the food service area. Guests may also use a library area, which includes a sampling of periodicals and books.

The use of plush but traditional seating, soft colors and mahogany accents unifies the public space. These themes continue in the 187 guest rooms. Function is important in the rooms as well. As an example, the designers provided for a telephone on the large writing desk as well as on the night-stand. The peach and green palette of the rooms gives them a refreshing look year-round.

Green marble flooring, used in the Compri's multi-use public space, directs the traffic flow and adds a note of luxury.

Meeting rooms continue the peach and green color scheme used throughout the hotel. The line of the chairs, tie-back draperies and chandelier highlight the property's traditional character.

Flowing under fluttering banners, the pool is flanked by traditional columns and a window wall to integrate with the overall interior design.

STOUFFER CONCOURSE HOTEL

Location: LOS ANGELES, CALIFORNIA, USA
Hotel Company: STOUFFER HOTELS CORP.
Interior Design: BARRY DESIGN (PUBLIC AREAS/GOVERNOR'S
                   SUITES); STOUFFER HOTELS CORPORATION
                   (GUEST ROOMS, SUITES)
Architecture: GIN WONG & ASSOCIATES

Airport hotels, as a category, are known more for their function than their form. Stouffer Concourse Hotel is among the stylistically rare and welcome exceptions.

"We wanted to design a hotel that would keep guests coming back—not just for a place to sleep—but to enjoy the restaurants and ballroom, in fact, the overall atmosphere," said Los Angeles-based designer Robert Barry.

One aspect of the design solution was to personalize the hotel's larger spaces and give each a sense of identity. An elegance pervades the lobby and lounge areas, thanks to daylight colors and the arrangement of sofas and chairs into tete-a-tete seating areas. Though marbled walls and pillars open up the space with an impressive verticality, low dividers and strategic planters create a private sub-strata that invites guests to linger.

Many of these elements are translated through other materials into the scheme for the Charisma Cafe, the hotel's three-meal-a-day restaurant. Although the space is definitely "California casual," it retains high quality appeal. It features custom marble countertops, as well as gold wall tiles and accents hand-stenciled with gold leafing.

Checkerboard marble leads into the specialty restaurant, Trattoria Grande. Starting with a neon sign that highlights the entry to the glass block front walls, the guest moves into the main dining area—a study in black and gold. The drama is heightened by ambient lighting from marble sconces, artwork, and exquisite examples of etched glass.

Despite the two-story sweep of this restaurant space, details direct the eye to more comfortable levels—from the hangng vines of the balcony to the strategically placed vases and tactile curves of the custom marble counter.

Casino Hotels

Dirk Obliers   Larry E. Seitz

*P*erhaps in no other segment of the hotel industry is "hyperbole" more evident and acceptable than in a casino hotel. Unlike most hotel design, casino designers are not looking to create a "home away from home," but rather a fantasy world.

According to Larry E. Seitz, the president of L.E. Seitz Associates, Inc., "Gaming, like any other adult leisure activity is, in essence, an escape to another life. The accomplishment of the visual portion of this transport is the direct responsibility of the casino designer who must create an eating, sleeping, entertainment, and gaming facility that is an environment of total escape."

Dirk Obliers, the "initiator" and creative head of the Rosenthal Hotel Design Team concurs, "The guest should experience a world that will certainly not be familiar to him, and leave with a sense of having experienced something new." Obliers introduced the successful concept of creating "artist" rooms in the Rosenthal Casino at Selb. Such famous craftsmen as Bjorn Wiinbland (Denmark), Paolozzi (England), Morandini (Italy), Dorothy Hafner (USA), and others were invited to choose the color schemes and provide the artwork. "The Rosenthal artists' rooms are successful examples of our endeavor to use contemporary means to escape uniformity," he explained.

Not too long ago, a casino operator's bottom line was profit at all cost. Guest comfort was often secondary as long as the dice were rolling and slot machines ringing. Says Seitz, "One day someone awoke with the idea that a lot of games in a semi-empty gaming house was not as profitable as slightly fewer games heavily used in an inviting environment. Operators now demand a total pack-age of design and function. Happily, there now exists a partnership between operators and designers that enhances the success of each partner, and ultimately the experience of the player."

Both Seitz and Obliers agree that "theme" plays a major role in design. Obliers observes, "Replacing old furnishings with new ones is not our concern, but rather the development of a particular theme which then must be interpreted by good, contemporary design. The procedure is always the same—first the theme and then the design solution." Seitz notes, "Themed casinos that make strong, positive design statements are proving more and more successful.

As the number of casinos around the world continues to expand, more diversification in games and design will unite to enhance an even more altered state in design."

SANDS HOTEL & CASINO

Location: SAN JUAN, PUERTO RICO
Hotel Company: PRATT HOTEL CORP.
Interior Design: L.E. SEITZ ASSOCIATES, INC.
Architecture: RAY, MELENDEZ ASSOCIATES

In designing for the Sands in San Juan, the challenge was to renovate a derelict, bankrupt hotel into an amalgamation of cultures from all the tropical zones. "A potpourri of exotic arts and accessories related by the common thread of all the tropics creates our motif," claims Larry Seitz.

The evidence begins at the very entrance, with carved walls from a Himalayan wedding temple, carved elephant wedding panels from India, a pair of milk marble temple lions from Imperial China, and carvings from the Royal Palace of Bali.

As with most casino design where "exaggeration" is the norm, the casino's center Italian crystal chandelier is longer than a bowling alley. The 10,000 square foot casino is the largest in Puerto Rico.

Interiors were planned as beautiful rooms first, and then as showcases of glamour and excitement for gaming. Bolae Studios, the only glass artists in the U.S. who design for France's Baccarat Crystal, designed and produced the carved color art glass decoration found in the gaming areas.

A sinuous chandelier in the casino adds pizzaz to the slot machine and blackjack table area. Carved glass room dividers give a sense of privacy to the "high-roller" patrons in the Baccarat room.

Strategically placed palms and brass flamingos enhance this dining area while mellow tones of pale green and peach soothe the eye in this tropical setting.

Exotic ivory dragon and ram sculptures are reflected in the glass screen embellished with painted palms. The black-and-white fabric of the sofa with an orchid design adds an oriental flair to this guest room.

A large brass serpent surrounded by tropical foliage adds a Garden of Eden effect to a coral-toned, floral guest room.

Oriental touches accent this
black-and-white octagonal
private dining room through
use of a lily chandelier and
carved glass mirror. The table
setting is enhanced by a fresh
orchid arrangement designed
to match two-toned napkins.

THE TROPICANA
HOTEL & CASINO

Location:	ATLANTIC CITY, NEW JERSEY, USA
Hotel Company:	RAMADA, INC.
Interior Design:	MIRAGLIA DSGNTeĊ
Photography:	BILL BLIZZARD

Imagine turning an entire floor of standard guest rooms into one luxurious four-room suite. The intention in designing the "Dynasty Suite" in the Tropicana, was to create a sumptuous environment to indulge the high-rolling casino patron. With the image of "Alexis Carrington Colby," an aura of over-stated elegance permeates each area within the suite.

Entering the entry foyer the guest is surrounded by two-toned seafoam and lavender walls and carpets enhanced by a hand-carved English "Twig" mirror and a self-playing white Sammick Baby Grand Piano.

As one enters into the living room, complete with billowing balloon-swag gracing the windows, one's view is immediately directed to the custom-imported Italian marble tile wet bar accented by Art Deco stools.

A feeling of sensual pleasure and relaxation is created in the Jacuzzi room by a rippling Italian fountain adjacent to a bathtub, adorned with solid gold faucets and two Temple Dragon sculptures.

Whether it is the surrounding lush foliage or the soft plush carpeting throughout, the "Dynasty Suite" embraces its guests in unparalleled comfort after a day of playing at high stakes.

Walking into this bedroom one is awed by the fully upholstered king-size bed, complete with a full plate glass mirror overhead and surrounded by elegant seafoam and lavender fabric swags. Imported Chinese nightstands feature a classic bamboo wrap with brass hardware and corners.

In the Jacuzzi Room, a "super bath," with solid gold faucets, is located next to a grand Italian fountain combining the comfort of water jets in the Jacuzzi and the calm trickle of water from the fountain to please the senses totally.

The most striking features of the living room/wet bar area are the custom hand-etched, floral pattern mirrorwork in two panels. Foliage surrounds the self-contained, electric, solid concrete fountain, imported from Italy.

THE ROSENTHAL CASINO

Location: SELB, WEST GERMANY
Interior Design: ROSENTHAL AG
                     CREATIVE-TEAM/HOTEL DESIGN

The single most striking aspect of the Rosenthal Casino in Selb, West Germany, is its "artists" guest rooms. The design team at Rosenthal AG wanted to create an environment with discernible character through use of experimental and consistently modern design.

To accomplish this, fourteen prominent artistic craftsmen from around the world were each invited to choose the color scheme for a room. They were charged with selecting the color tones for the walls, furniture, window treatment and "Artist's Niche" where their own artwork would be showcased.

Lino Sabattini from Italy chose soft gray and blue tones. His black porcelain "Porcelaine noire" graces the entrance. Johan van Loon of the Netherlands leaned toward pastels to showcase his light, transparent "Pergament Porcelain." The pop-art room by Eduardo Paolozi of Great Britain is highlighted with light blue, yellow and turquoise to set off his "DOG 2000" art piece.

The challenge they all faced and met was to offer innovative ideas, creativity and surprising solutions—without compromising their individuality—to create their own unmistakable "worlds." Even the most conservative of guests have expressed a positive reaction to this unique and avant-garde design approach.

Black and white were the preferred colors of Dorothy Hafner from the USA to showcase her "Flash" wall art.

Michael Boehm of Germany chose to display his glass-etching talent in the room divider of his "artist" room.

LAS VEGAS
HILTON

Location: LAS VEGAS, NEVADA USA
Hotel Company: HILTON HOTELS CORP.
Interior Design: KOVACS AND ASSOCIATES
Architecture: RISSMAN & RISSMAN

In a city where night never meets day and individuals are absorbed into a glittering, surreal universe of fantasy, the Las Vegas Hilton offers a world of traditional comfort and elegance. On the 29th floor of this "megalopolis" of over 3,000 rooms, among them 274 suites, one finds the nine super-suites that suspend reality.

These residences of pure luxury and opulence were designed primarily for high-rolling clients. Each suite, denoting a different theme, covers an area of approximately 3,000-3,700 square feet.

The "Regal Suite," set in tones of honey and cream, is monochromatic. It offers coziness and charm with an Oriental touch. A sparkling crystal chandelier sets off the dining and wet bar areas, with foliage and fresh flowers adding touches of color.

For those wishing to be carried back to the golden era of Hollywood in the '30s there is the "Hollywood Suite." In the living room area, four eye-catching tables—from spiralled black and rectangular glass to zig-zag metal—add both function and artistic flair to the black and white surroundings. Geometric detailing in the arches is softened by the warm glow of indirect lighting from wall sconces. Tones of gray and lavender in the wall treatment and carpeting are enhanced by the rich-toned black and white design of overstuffed pillows resting on plush sofas.

Each of the nine super-suites offers its own characteristic ambience to tease any individual taste.

Stark geometric lines in the living room of the "Hollywood Suite" are reminiscent of the early contemporary style found in Hollywood of the '30s. Satin pillows enhance the black velvet sofa adding splash to the gray-toned room. Stepped molding and silver columns add a "picture-frame" effect to the view of the "City of Glitter."

Pure sensual luxury permeates the bath area in the "Bedroom Suite." The raised marbled platform embraces a round sunken bathtub as the circular lines of the ceiling mirror add symmetry to the room. A tulip-shaped mirror behind the tub gives a headboard effect while serving as a room divider.

Straightback upholstered honey-gold chairs surround the glass dining table in the "Hollywood Suite." Additional accents are found in the tiled floor design and black pillars supporting sculptures which flank the large wall painting.

A gold-toned swag envelopes
the four-poster bed in the
"Regal Suite." Interesting to
note is the incorporation of
the bathing area with the
bedroom itself—a throwback
to the days of ancient Rome.
Fresh flowers and subtle lighting add a feeling of romance
to this royal sleeping area.

TRUMP'S CASTLE HOTEL AND CASINO

Location:	ATLANTIC CITY, NEW JERSEY, USA
Interior Design:	KOVACS AND ASSOCIATES
Architecture:	JOHN CARL WARNECKE, F.A.I.A.

Frequent gaming patrons, be they in Las Vegas or Atlantic City, find it easy to lose their "sense of place." Too often the public and gaming areas of casino hotels start to look alike. The repetitive color schemes of red, blue, green and turquoise can be found in most gambling establishments.

This is not the case at Trump's Castle... One of the major requests by Trump management was subtlety, not only in design, but in color. Consequently, rich earth tones of sienna, brown and gold, were selected to add a feeling of relaxation and to promote identity.

The interior does reflect an appealing dichotomy of design from the flashiness of the lobby ceiling with its overwhelming 300-foot lighting fixture, to the soothing ambience of the lounge areas.

According to Zoltan Kovacs, designing for casino hotels can get the creative juices flowing. One can pull out all the stops and allow the imagination to run wild. The appeal of Trump's Castle is this intriguing mesh of flamboyance and class.

Thus, here is a hotel which dares to be unconventional by using neutrals to neutralize and hot colors common to casinos.

What would a casino hotel be without lights? From the mammoth 300-foot light fixture to the illumination of the grand staircase, one can make no mistake that they are in the Trump's Castle.

Subtle tones of sienna, brown and gold in the upholstery, carpeting and support columns give the gaming room a distinctive look

Royal tones of blue, from the carpeting to the chairs, contrasted by the wall glass outlined in gold brass, present an atmosphere of regal splendor to the high-stakes gaming patron in the Baccarat Room.

THE WILLARD INTER—CONTINENTAL
PENINSULA HOTEL HONG KONG
JEFFERSON SHERATON HOTEL
EQUINOX HOUSE HOTEL
GRAND HOTEL
CHATEAU LAURIER

Robert Lush

Peter Rice

*E*xpert hotel restoration is a rich blend of hard work and art work, extensive research and expansive creativity.

Designers who win commissions to restore the glory of grand hotels are able to work in some of the most beautiful buidings in the world. Many of the structures included in this chapter were designed as showplaces where the haute monde could see and be seen.

Many of them also shared a common fate. As styles and cities changed and antique became synonymous with unprogressively "old fashioned," these properties began a decline that sent some perilously close to the wrecker's ball:

Because these restorations are businesses, not museums, they had to be faithful but practical. As Robert Lush, chairman of London-based Richmond Design Group says, "There are two types of restoration: One is strictly academic, and the money invested is for academic or historic reasons; the other is not only to restore a style, but to make a building work."

"Modern services have to be intro-duced without spoiling the hotel's ambience. Where new work is carried out, it must be done in a style and with materials that may not be original but must be consistent with the original design," stresses Lush.

Designers also must draw on the services of the small number of trades people who know how to restore the balustrades, moldings and plaster details that make these hotels works of art. "Finding trades people skilled in restoration techniques can be very difficult. Many of the trades involved are dying art forms," comments Peter Rice, of Toronto-based Rice Brydone Limited. However, in the UK and Europe, these highly-specialized trades are beginning to attract young artisans.

But the result is worthwhile, both for hotelier and guest. Heather Jones, of Rice Brydone Limited, points out, "Guests staying in renovated hotels experience the best of both worlds, old and new. They have all of the modern amenities and safety features in the elegance of an "old world" setting. Today's guests are charmed by the sense of history that distinguishes an older bilding from chain hotels."

THE WILLARD INTER-CONTINENTAL

Location: WASHINGTON, D.C.
Hotel Company: INTER-CONTINENTAL HOTELS
Interior Design: TOM LEE LTD.
Architecture: VLASTIMIL KOUBEK
Photography: PETER AARON/ESTO

Successful restoration involves not only choosing pieces of furniture appropriate for a certain era or matching antique wallcoverings, it also hinges upon recreating the spirit of a hotel in its heyday.

Sarah Tomerlin Lee, head of New York-based Tom Lee Ltd., expertly addressed both of these challenges in her restorative design for the Willard Inter-Continental. Working under guidelines from the Pennsylvania Avenue Development Corp. which mandated the retention of 1904 color schemes and architectural back-grounds, Lee and architect Vlastimil Koubek breathed grand new life into a property rumored to be a prospective victim for conversion or demolition.

A key element of the lobby decor was its ceiling, once accented by the seals of the 45 states in the union at that time. Sold long before the restoration, they were recovered, and repainted by hand in a labor of love that required more than two years.

Antique furnishings are mixed with accurate reproductions throughout the public spaces. Old and new are unified by the color schemes of the era—particularly the rose and gold tones of the lobby. Wood panels and millwork are dark, usually warmed by the glow of graceful chandeliers.

Oriental-inspired carpets are a design link throughout the public spaces of the 365-room hotel. Gilded tones, with olive and scarlets pre-dominating, match the color ways of 1904. The intricate patterns of these accent carpets are played up against solid color pattern-on-pattern or multi-colored striped upholstery fabric.

Modeled after the check-in desks of the 1900s, this concierge's station is topped with marble that blends with the golden tones of the lobby. The new registration desk was moved to another corner and masks an up-to-the-minute computerized check in/check out system.

Cascading chandeliers and
ornate ceiling details give the
Crystal Room a magnificent
verticality that befits a space
used to entertain heads of
state.

A circular motif spirals down from the ceiling through the lines of the rich wood bar and its gleaming brass rail. Wall booths and windows trimmed in olives and golds serve as the perfect frame.

Banquet rooms are usually a design afterthought, but the fine murals, crystal chandeliers and Oriental-patterned carpets make the Willard's ballroom elegant enough to be a centerpiece of the opulent hotel.

PENINSULA HOTEL HONG KONG

Location: HONG KONG
Hotel Company: PENINSULA GROUP
Interior Design: BENT SEVERIN & ASSOCIATES
Architecture: BENT SEVERIN & ASSOCIATES

Hotel designers who embark on restoration must expect the unexpected. But even veteran designers admit that it's difficult to anticipate all of the pitfalls they will face.

The legendary Peninsula Hotel in Hong Kong is a case-in-point example of the risks and rewards of renovations. Like all major hotel undergoing design work, it had to remain open during its rejuvenation. It would have been unthinkable to close its lobby—one of the premier meeting places in Hong Kong. The answer was to schedule construction around peak traffic or sleeping hours, which meant that work was limited to less than six hours a day.

Designers with Bent Severin & Associates, with offices in the Far East and the USA, were also faced with the bane of all restoration—the layers of previous designs. Since few records of the hotel's mechanical or architectural plans remained, the designers and architects could only guess at what was behind the existing walls and ceilings. They found that floors that were believed to be solid were actually timber floors and timber beams. Walls encased two, three or four layers of various construction styles. Ceilings were layered over other ceilings, in some cases three deep. By carrying out the restoration in small areas, the complete restoration of the hotel was achieved within two years.

The rejuvenated Peninsula features traditional English styling that reflects Hong Kong's history and underscores a residential feeling. This home-away-from-home look was particularly important since many of the hotel's guests travel long distances and stay three nights or more.

Though an English traditional style predominates the design of public spaces and guest rooms, the designers created a special contemporary, Oriental flavor for the Spring Moon Chinese specialty restaurant. The strong lines of the architecture contrast with the curves of the tables and chairs.

European elegance and the delicate intricacy of Oriental styling blend in this stately dining area of the Marco Polo Suite.

Rare archive photographs were used to create the delicate 19th century French-style floral pattern used for the guest room's bedspreads and draperies. Burl and teak wood furnishings, with brass trim, complement the fabric's olive and terra cotta tones.

JEFFERSON SHERATON HOTEL

Location:	RICHMOND, VIRGINIA, USA
Hotel Company:	SHERATON CORPORATION
Interior Design:	HOCHHEISER-ELIAS DESIGN GROUP INC.
Architecture:	VLASTIMIL KOUBEL
Photography:	WHITNEY COX

The design challenge for the restoration of the Jefferson Sheraton was clear: Maintain historic authenticity in this certified, landmark building, but redesign the space to function as a modern hotel.

Achieving this sometimes contradictory goal required careful coordination by designers with Hochheiser-Elias, headquartered in New York City. As an example, the chandeliers and sconces add period elegance to the colonnade framing the grand staircase, but high tech lighting was integrated into existing plasterwork to provide proper illumination. As in Thomas Jefferson's day, custom carpet which defines seating areas in the impressive main rotunda can be rolled up to create space for dances or parties.

License was taken with some details, points out designer Brad Elias. "The original reception area included pits with live alligators. We kept the pits, but represented the alligators with bronze sculptures."

In the Lemaire restaurant and cocktail lounge, the service bars and waitress stations required for this 130-seat area were integrated into niches and alcoves so as not to interfere with the historically accurate interior architecture.

The style throughout the hotel is American Renaissance. In the executives suites, this theme is scaled down to fit a private space but is no less impressive. Original antiques, statuary, and—in suites with fireplaces—andirons, discovered during the restoration, provide period authenticity. Although some contemporary design elements were introduced into some suites, the color scheme of mint, rose, fawn and black keeps a consistent look for these spaces.

The grand stairway of the Jefferson Sheraton, the model for Tara in "Gone With The Wind," spills down to a main floor rotunda which can be quickly cleared of furnishings and carpets for dances and parties.

Informal food services areas are tucked into irregularly shaped spaces under the lobby balcony. Operable beveled glass doors, fitted into the architectural openings, provide easy access and fulfill the operator's mandate that all food service areas must be lockable.

A statue of Thomas Jefferson presides over a classical and neutral lobby, highlighted by the artistry of exquisite stained glass windows and a breathtaking rotunda dome.

Furnishings in a modified American Federal style reflective of the hotel's public spaces were used in both the guest rooms and suites. Modern climate control and fire-safety systems were integrated into the style without eliminating architectural details such as windows or fireplaces.

Thomas Jefferson's acquaintance with French culture inspired the grandeur of this function room. Its fleur-de-lis patterned carpet complements the grid of the ornate ceiling and its sparkling chandeliers. This opulent framework complements a variety of table arrangements and color combinations.

Since no modification could be made to the elegant scagliola columns in the lobby, the designer used them as dividers to lend added privacy to T.J.'s Cafe while still providing a lovely view.

EQUINOX HOUSE HOTEL

Location: MANCHESTER VILLAGE, VERMONT, USA
Interior Design: DOROTHY DRAPER
Architecture: EINHORN YAFFEE PRESCOTT,
                   ARCHITECTURE & ENGINEERING P.C.
Photography: BILL MURPHY/JOSEPH SCHULYER/DUPONT

Once a stopping point for four U.S. Presidents and the summer home of Mrs. Abraham Lincoln, the Equinox House Hotel was closed in 1974 and lay dormant for 10 years. It took a US$3.4 million grant, supplemented by preservation tax incentives, to create enough financial support for a US$20 million restoration program to revitalize this landmark property.

Not surprisingly, the structural foundations of the nearly 200-year-old core buildings had deteriorated severely and had to be supported. Design work began with the recording of historic architectural fabric for rehabilitation, where it was possible, or replication, where it was not. Most of the exterior aspects of the four classically-styled wood frame buildings, unified by a monumental two-story colonnade, was in good enough condition to be restored. The interiors, however, were candidates for rehabilitation.

The trick for Carlton Varney, of New York City-based Dorothy Draper, was to make the interiors look "as if they'd merely undergone a cosmetic over-haul." For that reason, he turned to the bright greens and reds used around the turn of the century to enliven elegant hotels. He also kept accessories simple because the Equinox rose to fame as a summer resort—though now it will be used year-round both as a resort and conference center.

Architecture becomes art in the curves of this spiral staircase which leads from the lobby to the second floor. In the guest rooms, colors are bright and patterns restrained to underscore the airy elegance of what once was, and is again, one of Vermont's premier resorts.

Though the Equinox had fallen prey to time and vandalism, some details, including this original fireplace from 1832 in the tavern, remain.

Close attention was paid to all aspects of the hotel including that graceful intersection of columns with the lobby's curved ceiling.

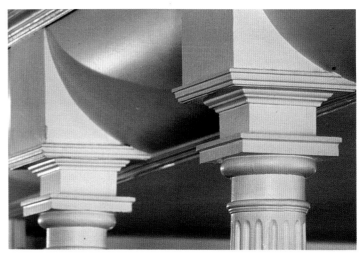

Bright flowers bloom on the lobby carpet, contrasting with a rich black background. Columns and walls—white, pristine—fit the hotel's idyllic resort setting.

GRAND HOTEL

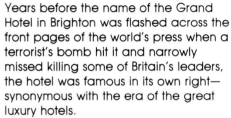

Location:	BRIGHTON, ENGLAND
Hotel Company:	DE VERE HOTELS
Interior Design:	RICHMOND DESIGN GROUP

Years before the name of the Grand Hotel in Brighton was flashed across the front pages of the world's press when a terrorist's bomb hit it and narrowly missed killing some of Britain's leaders, the hotel was famous in its own right—synonymous with the era of the great luxury hotels.

Since the damage of the bombing was so extensive, De Vere executives decided to rejuvenate nearly all of the hotel's interiors. They invested US$20 million, with US$3.74 million set aside for interior design.

Important elements, such as a breathtaking cast iron central staircase, were preserved and used to set an appropriate design theme for a 19th Century hotel. "All previous modern alterations were removed from the public areas and the elegant original relief work and design were restored," points out Richmond Design's Robert Lush.

However, some amenities were added to extend the hotel's appeal. An enclosed balcony replaced a terrace formerly open to the sea so that the restaurant and bar could be used year-round. Also, the rooms overlooking the sea were enlarged by narrowing the corridors to make them more comfortable and spacious. Guest bathrooms were sheathed in marble, and twin whirlpool baths were installed in the romantic suites.

The guest room color scheme focuses on muted harvest colors that provide visual warmth when contrasted with the frequently steel-gray sea.

Plaster and iron are worked into a delicate lacework effect that frames the entry to the Grand Hotel Brighton.

An elegantly etched glass divider screens off this dining area. Stately columns not only subdivide the space, but also frame an innovative buffet presentation.

Patterned wallcoverings provide an interesting backdrop for the bar's broken pediment mirror frames. It also completes the theme introduced in the intricately patterned carpet.

Design gives this smallish guest room big impact. The floral flounce of the canopy bed is mirrored by the balance of the draperies. Though patterns vary, their similar sizes and blue-and-gold color scheme visually expand the space.

CHATEAU LAURIER

Location: OTTAWA, CANADA
Hotel Company: CANADIAN PACIFIC HOTELS
Interior Design: RICE BRYDONE LIMITED
Architecture: CLARKE DARLING DOWNEY
Photography: ELAINE KILBURN

Some hotels are so much part of their community that the public develops a pride of ownership in them. One such case is the Chateau Laurier.

"We wanted to create a restoration that would support the public's sense of ownership," says Peter Rice, of Toronto-based Rice Brydone Limited. After all, this was a hotel that had housed heads of state who rode the Canadian National Railway as far back as 1912, as well as generations of hopeful newlyweds and gatherings of people celebrating business breakthroughs or personal milestones.

The restoration had to be both careful and caring—careful enough to add now-necessary life safety systems, and caring enough not to destroy the hotel's charm.

Original details, such as the lobby's oak panels and trim, travertine floor and fluid arches, were restored. A Victorian fountain was added for a touch of romantic elegance. Where restoration was impossible, reproduction moldings and plasterwork were created and worked into any fragments of the original that could be retained.

A grand stairway leads to a rediscovered mezzanine which now features meeting space stylistically integrated into the rest of the hotel. As an example, an 18-seat executive board room is enriched with silken panels and adds an elegant comfort with silk-upholstered chairs.

One of the few major changes was the addition of the glass-enclosed Zoe's conservatory. Working closely with the Ottawa Historical Society, the designers were able to recapture an authentic look. Low, curved rattan chairs are arranged around cast iron and glass tables to achieve an art nouveau ambience. Travertine and marble floors link this 120-space restaurant/lounge area with the neighboring public spaces.

The semicircular poufs of the tablecloth are mirrored by the graceful fan folding of the napkins. In every detail, the main dining room reinforces a look of turn-of-the-century elegance.

Aglow in candlelight colors and open enough to provide pre-function spaces, the Governor General's lobby services the meeting rooms on the "rediscovered" mezzanine level.

Wherever possible, the original plasterwork and molding of the 1912 lobby were retained or repaired. One of the few touches is the addition of a romantic Victorian fountain.

The registration area was moved to a quiet corner out of the main traffic flow so as not to steal drama from the lobby's grand entrance. The columns unify the design, while a curve of black marble masks updated front-desk operations.

Executive board rooms double as private dining rooms, which means that chairs must be comfortable both for long meetings or leisurely dinners. The patterned section of the carpet helps draw the focus to the center of the room, making the space seem larger and airier.

CHAPTER **6**

Renovation

Glenn Texeira

*R*enovation is the blood and guts of hotel interior design. Every chapter in this volume has renovation.

The down and dirty work can make or break a designer's reputation. In some hotels there can be no changes in exterior or interior architecture, and the designer who accepts the commission is immediately handicapped by an unmoveable famine of spatial choices.

Yet the designer is expected to update the hotel, perhaps change its image, and make the renovation so magnificent that a roadside motel will rival the de luxe grand hotels of the world.

One of these realists is Glenn Texeira of Project Associates, Los Angeles, California, USA. Here's his first body punch to the designer who is dreaming of rose colored wine glasses: "The important task is meeting tough building and safety requirements." And this must be done in the framework of the ". . . integrity of the original architecture."

That integrity must be kept while replacing ancient plumbing, rewiring dated electrical systems, installing central air conditioning, and adding mandated sprinklers.

On the design side, Texeira begins with this philosophy: "Create a harmony between past and present by knowing what to respect in the ambience of a bygone era, and then walk a fine line regarding what to remove."

His next punch is to remind the inexperienced designer that he can't go it alone. He calls renovation "(often). . . a unique partnership between the architectural and design teams. . .," and expands that cooperation to include "the crafts people hired to restore finishes and murals."

Some renovations aren't delicate at all. They were, as Texeira admits, "built to last." But they "sit on property sites that demand the highest commercial rates, requiring extra millions of investment. In these, the designer—to insure profitability—must renovate to convert a hotel into luxury suites with fewer rooms, or a luxury hotel into one with more rooms.

BILTMORE HOTEL

Location: CORAL GABLES, FLORIDA, USA
Interior Design: LYNN WILSON ASSOCIATES
Photography: FRANCETIC PHOTO ASSOCIATES, INC.

Groin vaulting of Moorish design is awesome in this columned lobby with its hanging and wrought iron plant stands.

It was a grand hotel, the old Biltmore in Coral Gables, Florida, USA. It was designed in the '20s by Schultze and Weaver, a fantastic amalgam of Spanish, Moorish and Beaux Arts influences, centered about a 315-foot tower replicating the Giralda in Seville, Spain.

Then, during World War II, it was turned over to the military for use as a hospital. Government standards had no room for elaborately painted ceilings, floors of marble and parquet, or French doors. The ceiling was transformed into a white plain, floors were covered with black linoleum, windows were reconfigured to accommodate aluminum frames, and rooms were partitioned and given flourescent fixtures.

Later, the building was abandoned for 20 years to the termites, cock-roaches and pigeons. The grand hotel was dead, so dessicated it wasn't worth the honorable burial of the wrecker's ball.

Suddenly, the designers were called in and told, "You have four days to give us plans to return the queen to her throne."

The desire was to rebuild the hotel to its glory. New dining and ballroom facilities had to be developed within public areas that could not, for historical integrity, be spatially altered. Only the second-floor lobby remained intact.

Both guest wings were razed to the shell, and the original 350 rooms reduced to 285. Throughout the hotel new French doors and windows were installed to the tune of US$1 million.

There was not adequate documenta-tion on which to base restoration work. The lobby ceiling was a disaster: but the designer found a few specks of paint left in corners and some old sepia photographs of the original patterning. Microscopic analysis allowed a team of 35 Mexican ecclesiastical restorers to renovate the lobby's walls and ceilings.

Intricately carved, high backed chairs with low seats are characteristic of antique Spanish design.

Restoration of ceilings and mouldings is carefully emphasized by muting the elegant chairs with dark green plush fabric. Chair backs repeat the floral pattern.

This cafe with its fabulous wooden ceilings has its design ancestry in a kind of light-hearted Early American style.

GROVE PARK INN
& COUNTRY CLUB

Location: ASHEVILLE, NORTH CAROLINA, USA
Interior Design: DESIGN CONTINUUM
Architecture: DANIEL INTERNATIONAL
Photography: JOHN GRUNKE

Grove Park was built in 1913 with huge fireplaces, specially-built furniture and imported soft goods—a dream inn designed without the benefit of a professional architect.

Since then, it's housed many Presidents of the United States. It's on the National Register of public places—but it was showing its age.

The renovators had not only to redo the public and private areas of the 200-room original hotel within historic specifications, but to add a new wing of approximately 200 rooms.

It took four years to complete. Restoration was generally difficult, but the renovation made use of a lot of modern processes. For example, many original woods were fumed oak, a process in which the wood is darkened by ammonia vapors. This technique is no longer in use, so hand-rubbed stains were used to approximate it.

Other deviations included duplicating dining room oak chairs, but enlarging them for guests' comfort. Some new pieces had to be invented in the spirit of the originals. After careful study, the designer had to create new carpets to match the old motif.

The new wing steps off eight floors below the old, down the side of the mountain, with a stone facade in keeping with the original stone masonry.

This was a monumental interiors program, a combination of restoration and renovation, but with the complication of a new building to be "renovated" to be in the character of the old.

It is a marvelous example of the Arts & Crafts period in American design.

A subtle Oriental theme begins with a Chinese wall hanging, and continues with Chinese lantern lighting inside a wooden breakfront in this multi-level dining area.

This banquet room features drop lighting and a painted glass behind the dais.

Faithful in spirit to 1913 style is this simple oak table that is the concerige's desk of the new wing. Beyond the railing is a stairway that leads down to an indoor swimming pool.

HOTEL
D'ANGLETERRE

Location: COPENHAGEN, DENMARK
Interior Design: WILSON-GREGORY-AEBERHARD
Photography: ROBERT MILLER

Sometimes a design commission sounds only a little out of the ordinary: take a European hotel, renovate 71 guest rooms creating one room out of what were formerly two, and redo the bar, restaurant and lobby lounge.

The name is the Hotel D'Angleterre in Copenhagen, reputed to be the oldest hotel in Europe! Now the excitement turns to awe, and the designer is particularly "honored" to have been chosen.

The rooms are all suites, with a blue scheme created to provide a dramatic feel. A specially designed custom screen separates beds and seating groups. The accents are in golds, and the furniture recreates the style of 200 years ago, when the hotel first opened. The furniture far antecedes the Danish modern that became contemporary in the '50s.

Some of the hotel's lost splendor is recaptured by specially designed high-gloss brown walnut casegoods. Larger rooms have marble baths with huge walnut-framed mirrors and simple, straight-line brass shower fixtures of extremely charming design.

On one of Copenhagen's most beautiful squares, the D'Angleterre has a history of being part of important political and social events: the home away from home for royalty, ministers, and artists of renown.

Those artists would have admired the custom-designed etched glass panel in the renovated dining room, framed by armoire-style wine racks.

The renovation is rich-looking everywhere, as befits what many believe is the most ancient of all European hotels. Within a framework of the US$1.2 million budget, this renovation displays both the designer's pride in being selected, and a pride in the ultimate execution.

Marble bathroom makes clever use of highly polished brass from the door handle and faucets to the charming shower fixtures. The double sink and huge mirror underscore its elegance.

Armoire-style wine racks frame the custom-painted blue glass in the dining room, while highly polished wooden chairs are upholstered vertically in dark red associated with the Tudor period.

Uncommon in a hotel where a blue theme predominates, this red motif with green highlights is beautiful with a coverlet that matches the curtains and the curved valances. Wood tables with gold trim are affectionately counterpointed by a modern glass table with gold supports.

INN AT THE OPERA

Location:	SAN FRANCISCO, CALIFORNIA, USA
Interior Design:	PROJECT ASSOCIATES, INC.
Architecture:	PROJECT ASSOCIATES, INC.

Rejuvenation swept through San Francisco's Van Ness Corridor, and the Inn at the Opera was in its way. "Goodbye" was the future of this Victorian structure. But in four months, it became "hello."

In the course of renovation, the project actually required new floors and new roofs. The work was drastic. Within one area 135 feet by only 18 feet, a whole new environment was created as an example of how the Victorian heritage of San Francisco can be respected without creating a heavy period piece.

The garage was leveled. So were the basement and adjacent liquor store. All that was left was a stairway and an elevator shaft.

Now guests sail through an entrance of bright marble and brass, greeted by a turn-of-the-century reception area. A palette of pale celadon and rose surrounds antique area carpets. Then on to the lounges, and dining areas, with mahogany bars and carved wood chairs.

Intimate conversation may be snuggled in sumptuous sofas, highlighted by tapestry pillows. Although some walls are painted a rich chestnut, others are upholstered in French tapestry. The bar is warmed by a veined marble fireplace.

In the 48 guest suites there are comfortable stuffed chairs, classic European furniture, and windows with pulled-back, fringed draperies. The theme in the bedrooms is fanciful, floral and contrasts with the muted pastels of the non-sleeping areas of each suite.

Not only did the designer succeed with a building he admits "...was better suited for a demolition ball than a design plan," but he was called in very late—after the owners decided against continuing with the original design firm.

The Inn at the Opera now anchors the Van Ness Corridor, instead of letting it drift away.

Muted pastel colors give way to large floral prints as you enter the bedroom portion of the suites. Not shown are the French doors.

A French-style chair used in this design was found frequently in Victorian bedrooms. The fringed curtains with drop valances recreate the elegance of old San Francisco.

Merely the corner of a lounge area, the rich woods and tables covered with cloths make it look like a fine old English club.

These broad, rich floral prints and highly polished woods near the veined-marble fireplace are the focal point of the lounge.

WESTIN HOTEL CALGARY

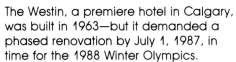

Location:	CALGARY, CANADA
Hotel Company:	WESTIN HOTELS & RESORTS
Interior Design:	FORMA
Architecture:	COHOS-EVAMY PARTNERSHIP
Photography:	EDEN ARTS

The Westin, a premiere hotel in Calgary, was built in 1963—but it demanded a phased renovation by July 1, 1987, in time for the 1988 Winter Olympics.

The project included the complete renovation of 395 guest rooms, suites, meeting rooms, the ballroom, public spaces and not less than four food and beverage outlets.

The concept of the renovation was to visually change and update it—a new and exciting energy was required.

The original lobby with its dated dark wood paneling, dark carpeting, and aging fixtures, was transformed into a contemporary design of travertine and glass. A glaze of light neutral wood coloring updated the rescuable portions of the old woodwork.

Throughout the project, Calgary's location on the Canadian plains is reflected in the palette: the colors are those of wheat, dried prairie grasses, pale terra cotta and sunset pinks.

Rich, earthy textures and natural fibers carry through this theme. But the furnishings are not "of a kind": they are an eclectic mix of contemporary shapes, traditional folk art inspired pieces, and "deco" (in areas such as the bar).

In time for the Olympics, this hotel with its once-heavy "old wagon wheels" look, became a bright and shining contemporary place more in keeping with the new pace of Western Canada.

Urns hold long branches of Canadian Plains brush to frame this highly contemporary tete-a-tete area. These are local rural colors, brought indoors.

Formerly a dark, heavy area,
this corner under the columns
has been brightened and
made more contemporary by
the eclectic mix of
upholstered sofas facing open
chairs.

This contemporary room in
gold and pink is accented
with flowers. Residential-style,
stuffed sofas replaced the
tired, "heavy looking" chairs.

From this view it's possible to see how much brightening has been added by turning the old, dark woods into light woods—accomplished with finishes, not by replacing the original wood with its excellent grain.

OMNI HOTEL, ST. LOUIS UNION STATION

Location: ST. LOUIS, MISSOURI, USA
Hotel Company: OMNI HOTELS
Interior Design: HELLMUTH, OBATA & KASSABAUM
Architecture: HELLMUTH, OBATA & KASSABAUM

In the American Middle West, huge cities developed where waterways met railroads: Cleveland, Chicago, Louisville and Minneapolis, to name a few. But among the most important was St. Louis, at the confluence of the Father of Waters and the wide Missouri.

In the old, typically American spirit of bigger and better, St. Louis' Union Station was built large enough to drill armies. Now that station, with its awesome arches and cathedral roof, is the Omni Hotel, so splendid in its execution that it is claimed "...Union Station will probably be the most important project of this century...the rest of the country will look at and be impacted by its renovation work."

In total, it's a vibrant mixed-use center. Outside, the Bedford limestone was restored to its turn-of-the-century glory. Then inside, the old ticket office, waiting room, offices, and train station restaurant, became the foundation of a 550-room luxury hotel.

The main lobby is accented with marble, stained glass and gold leaf, which recreates the original finish of the 65-foot barrel-vaulted ceiling. A lobby lounge and 100 rooms are located in the main station building. The hotel is completed by a 360,000 square-foot addition.

But it's the renovation (and necessary restoration) of the original headbuilding that is so inspiring.

This was once the world's busiest train station, and the largest single-span train shed ever built. The atrium is multi-floored with graceful, arched columns.

If ever a must-see hotel lobby existed, it's the huge Omni; the eye can't see it all at once. The renovator's design for the chairs and use of floor space was critical because of tremendous scope of the vault.

Entire hotels could fit inside the Omni's lobby.

Period pieces in blue (left) are turn-of-the-century replicas. Only a small part of the wall leading to the barrel arch is visible, as the scope of the lobby is on such a grand scale that the eye cannot take it all in at once.

BRACKNELL HILTON NATIONAL

Location:	BRACKNELL, ENGLAND
Hotel Company:	HILTON INTERNATIONAL
Interior Design:	TAVERN FURNISHING LIMITED

Blink and you might miss the renovation.

When the catastrophe of fire destroyed the public spaces and guest rooms of the Bracknell Hilton National, the TFL design team was beaten to the property only by the fire department.

The project director described the project as: "Fast track: an integrated interior design."

In eight weeks the hotel reopened to its guests—and not with the charred remains of disaster, but with seating and tables from Italy, fountains from Germany, wall coverings from the USA, and stained glass from Austria. The United Kingdom itself provided "specialist contracting," flooring, crafted joinery and counters.

The lobby has mirrored ceilings set off with columns, blonde caned chairs on a tiled floor, and recessed ceiling lighting augmented by ball lights atop tall brass standards.

The fluted columns are offset by thick plants, at the ceiling level. The check-in areas are tastefully downplayed and placed to one side. Light blue carpeting in heavy traffic areas is matched in the seat and back cushions of the chairs.

This delicate blue and white motif is broken only by the brass in the lighting and the cane of chairs. There is one blue upholstered central chair and sofa nest, but even this doesn't effect overall lightness and spaciousness of this space.

This remarkable renovation wasn't a case of "what can you do in eight weeks," but "do your best and have it done in eight weeks."

It is a tribute not only to exhaustive design, but to local workmen and craftsmen who helped put together the 120 rooms and public spaces that a mere two months before had been turned into charcoal.

Classical fluted columns combine with brass ball lamps to convey a modern, clean-line, airy elegance to the arriving guest.

Mirrored ceilings give a two-story effect to this corner of the lobby with its delicate electrics and wall hangings.

WESTIN ST. FRANCIS TOWER

Location: SAN FRANCISCO, CALIFORNIA, USA
Hotel Company: WESTIN HOTELS & RESORTS
Interior Design: FORMA
Photography: JOHN VAUGHAN

The complete renovation of 570 guest rooms and six hospitality suites in the Westin St. Francis Tower building isn't all the designer remembers: it's also those 27 floors of corridors.

It's that attention to detail that made this an excellent renovation. The original main hotel was built in 1904, but the contemporary Tower Building was erected in 1972.

Even though each room affords a spectacular view of the city, outdated design did little to enhance it. The designer decided to replace it and bring the tower into keeping with the main building.

A "classic but contemporary" style was created, by "careful use of colors and materials and a sensitive attention to existing architectural details."

New mouldings were installed, and old ones refinished, to reflect the quality and "old world" ambience of the main building. This was carried over into dropped valances and wood base-boards.

Because the narrow building was lined with columns of bay windows and generous ceiling heights, the designer recognized the opportunity to add character and individuality to these interior spaces.

Suites—six of them—are of a unique character. One, the Windsor Suite, was home to Queen Elizabeth and Prince Philip during their historic visit to San Francisco in 1983, and is appropriately designed—yet the Shangri-La suite reflects the strong Asian influence in the city's history.

In the corridors, the designer goes out of his way to report, "Custom corridor carpets were designed to echo the color and character of the lobby carpets, yet to reinterpret them in a more contemporary manner."

The eye of the good renovator misses nothing.

This delicate chandelier over the uncanopied four-poster mixes modern and Victorian. The armoire rests on delicate legs in the French style.

A painted screen forms the backdrop of this marvelously wood-accented room, in which the chair seats provide the only hint of fabric. The vase of flowers, and long tapirs, are focuses.

Solidly contemporary room looks out over San Francisco's night sky. The almost inevitable yellow tulips are fresh-picked.

MANDARIN ORIENTAL

Location: HONG KONG
Hotel Company: MANDARIN ORIENTAL
                   HOTEL GROUP
Interior Design: DON ASHTON (PUBLIC AREAS)

Renovation of Hong Kong's Mandarin Oriental (formerly The Mandarin) has just been completed, in time for the hotel's 25th anniversary.

It begins with a new-look facade of polished black granite from Angola, and a stainless steel canopy in gold, which opens onto a lobby. The hotel's original designer, Don Ashton, has given it a new look: the center of attention is in the new central walkway in white Carrera marble leading through luxurious carpeting to the grand staircase. Green onyx has been replaced with rare black marble as the backdrop for the hotel's much-loved Chinese carvings.

The renovated guest rooms have been refurbished to retain the traditional style of the Mandarin Oriental. Highlights include teak and burlwood paneling, Chinese porcelain lighting fixtures, beige wool carpets from New Zealand, and furnishings in "Chinoiserie," a style of chintz fabric copyrighted for Mandarin Oriental's exclusive use.

The bathrooms are now pale pink Portuguese marble floors and walls, with burgundy granite wash basins, chrome fittings and Chinese lacquered baskets.

Also part of the extensive renovation is the addition of a business center, which even offers secretarial service.

The hotel has a modern look, accented by its many Chinese objets d'art and traditional Asian materials such as marble and jade.

Smart-looking black lacquer faces overstuffed mauve in this inspiringly blended living room area of the Meiji Suite.

The bedroom portion of the
Meiji Suite is in blues, pinks
and purples, elegantly
contemporary in some
respects, but very Chinese in
others, such as its lacquered
wood.

DOUBLETREE-
NEW ORLEANS

Location: NEW ORLEANS, LOUISIANA, USA
Hotel Company: DOUBLETREE HOTELS
Interior Design: VIVIAN/NICHOLS ASSOCIATES, INC.
Photography: IRA MONTGOMERY

Although only 13 years old, the Doubletree-New Orleans was ready for a major renovation to bring it into the 1990s of interior design.

But it was to be done by reflecting the historical French perspective of a New Orleans location. The whole project was restrained by the costliness and impracticability of making any major architectural changes or relocating of spaces.

When it came to the lobby, lobby bar, restaurant, elevator cabs and second floor pre-function area, only four weeks were allowed between demolition and build-out.

The new flavor is more cultured and contemporary, residential in scale and French in taste.

The first floor public areas were visually opened with light beige walls and cream colored millwork, with travertine flooring materials. Contrast was added with deep green faux marble columns and richly patterned area rugs. Bleached wood tables and mirrors, and Louis XIV accent chairs, are French-inspired. Sofas are upholstered in deep blue and cranberry tapestry fabrics. Brass is introduced for a touch of shininess, as are large palms and other greenery. A magnificent tapestry is at the head of the grand staircase.

The restaurant has handpainted tiles whose design reflects the botanical imagery in its upholstery and window coverings.

In the 368 guest rooms, wall-to-wall French floral draperies add depth, while the fabric is repeated on the coverlet. The walls are cream, with taupe carpeting and a taupe plaid armchair contrasting to the deep fabric tones. The case pieces are an attractive blend in a natural fruitwood finish.

The Doubletree is an excellent example of the need to renovate even young hotels to keep up with the constant interior design ideas that attract guests.

Rich columns beneath twin arches frame the French decor of the new lobby, with its Louis XIV chairs and bleached wood tables.

The French theme carries on into the bar, where clean lines are accented by floral pieces and a baby grand piano.

Doubletree's restaurant has a remarkable feature: the very large inlaid red and white squares whose ancestry is, of course, the red and white checkered tableclothes of old French cafes.

WESTIN PASO DEL NORTE

Location: EL PASO, TEXAS, USA
Hotel Company: WESTIN HOTELS
Interior Design: WILSON & ASSOCIATES
Architecture: WILSON & ASSOCIATES
Photography: ROBERT MILLER

Lounge seating in tacked red leather is framed by restored Italian stained-glass windows which were part of original hotel.

Westin's Paso del Norte underwent a renovation that cost US$50 million, including the addition of a 17-story tower. It has a ballroom larger than a baseball infield.

But what the client wanted in this old hotel was a gutsy, Texas-style environment introduced into what was once a very ornate French hotel.

So the designers chose large scale furnishings which are "comfortable but not delicate." The original hotel lobby was transformed into the Dome Bar, and the original Tiffany glass dome was cleaned and restored.

The restaurant is a step into the past: elegant dining amid heavy taffeta fabrics on chairs and window treatments. Large bronze chandeliers hang over English Regency chairs. Accessories include English Adam-style antiques and artwork.

The reception table is Circa 1810, with gilded ram's heads, and the 18th century breakfront is inlaid with satinwood.

Italian craftsmen were contracted to create the beautiful scagliola work in rust and ochre. And the Tiffany dome was removed, piece by piece, and shipped to the restorer.

The stained glass in the dining room windows was Italian. Matching damaged pieces during its cleaning, repairing and reinstalling period, was extremely difficult.

The bare bulbs in the lobby bar are original; the hotel was one of the first buildings in El Paso to have electricity. Another design problem was designing around the marvelous, but massive, structural columns.

Today the Westin Paso del Norte is a magnificent tribute to the renovator's solutions when part of the work requires precise restoration.

Tiffany dome had to be removed piece by piece, sent away to be cleaned and restored, then reinstalled in a painstaking, time-consuming effort.

Massive columns in this three-meal restaurant were worked around beautifully to create intimate dining with a lot of natural lighting.

Flat, unpleated valance over curtains continues straight-line theme of huge armoire in this predominantly green guest room with its cream and reddish accents.

CINCINNATIAN HOTEL

Location: CINCINNATI, OHIO, USA
Interior Design: EDWARDS DESIGN GROUP
Photography: DAN FORER

The lobby is luxurious with its original marble grand stairway, coffered ceiling, and patterned marble floors. Dramatic use of lighting accentuates the classic use of pediments.

The Cincinnatian is more than 100 years old, a registered, historical landmark in this river town that calls itself the Queen City, being the "queen" of the Ohio River, one of America's most historic waterways.

Architecturally, the hotel is a miniature version of the famed Plaza in New York City. Its exterior remains intact, except for some new paint and windows, a fact of which Cincinnatians are proud: the town takes its history very seriously.

But the designer's objective inside was radical. It was to integrate the character of French Second Empire architecture into a 1980's luxury hotel.

It was highly successful, even though it was—not too long ago—a deteriorating property "heading for the wrecking ball." Its 300 rooms without private baths became 149 executive suites and luxury rooms with the amenities synonymous with deluxe.

An atmosphere of elegance and drama was achieved through use of a "timeless palette, material selection, and refined patterns that recall the Second Empire." Yet a setting was created that allowed the introduction of an avant-garde art collection.

The color palette in parts of the interior is beyond daring—or was several years ago when the use of purple and blue was not easy to sell to the ownership. But the design firm was extremely conscious of being involved with the prediction of color years in advance. By the time of completion, it was obviously correct.

Those are the kinds of predictions outstanding renovators must be able to make if they are to keep a hotel on the leading edge of interior design.

Every guest room (left) is different. This room has neo-classic overtones, patterned wall coverings, and traditional drapery treatments blended together in a scheme of purple and blue.

RADISSON HOTEL

Location: ST. PAUL, MINNESOTA, USA
Hotel Company: RADISSON HOTELS CORP.
Interior Design: CSA, INC.
Photography: LEA BABCOCK AND
GEORGE HEINRICH

The old Radisson in St. Paul has 482 guest rooms, and the renovator decided on a traditional theme to create a new image for a "tired, old hotel that was previously done in contemporary idiom."

The biggest problem was large spaces that were impersonal and devoid of character. Most were broken up and treated to architectural detailing. Because of the size of the hotel the renovation had to be phased over years.

Phase one was the lobby and lounge. Hard, cold, industrial materials were replaced with a soft, formal elegance, accomplished through an eclectic blend of French Empire, Oriental, and contemporary pieces, with the green, burgundy and mauve palette punctuated with accents of black lacquer.

Guest rooms and suites were made more residential, with the lobby palette reintroduced—this time, though, it's the burgundies and mauves that predominate, with marginal accent use of the greens.

The Radisson is one of the more traditional types of renovation: no architectural changes, but massive changes in ambience. It shows a new understanding of an old problem: "contemporary idiomatic" may not withstand the test of time, even over the short period of five or ten years. The designer takes a chance with his artistic expression. If the current idiom were Victorian, lucky; if it were Op Art, it may date itself quickly and never return, even as a curiosity.

Renovating into a traditional design is a growing trend among very large hotels, because the traditional style will still be valid over the several years it takes to do a phased renovation— today's Radisson will still be lovely when the guest rooms await the next round of renovations after the year 2000.

This renovated suite repeats the lobby idea of Oriental accents with its painted screen. Folding doors can separate sitting and dining areas. The design is very residential.

The 11 East Cafe features a Country French decor with a series of private dining rooms.

Beautiful Chinese screen on a black lacquered base made this once-impersonal lobby into an intimate and elegant public space for the arriving guest.

CHAPTER 7
All-Suites

Douglas L. Burbank

*W*here can you get two hotel rooms for the price of one? Nowadays the answer is simple—an "All-Suite" hotel. Not too long ago market studies were conducted to determine what amenities a traveler really did or did not want to have in a hotel. According to Douglas L. Burbank, a principal with Design Continuum, Inc., "In most markets, these surveys targeted the business traveler who has the potential of occupying sixty to seventy percent of available room nights. Customers for the remaining nights are primarily weekend travelers and families."

Research showed that those surveyed were interested in two things: 1) getting the most for their money at a minimum price; and 2) having a room where they could not only have sleeping accommodations but also conduct small meetings in a separate, enclosed area. Thus, the concept of the all-suite hotel

HILTON SUITES OF LEXINGTON GREEN

Location: LEXINGTON, KENTUCKY, USA
Hotel Company: HILTON HOTELS CORP.
Interior Design: DILEONARDO INTERNATIONAL, INC.
Architecture: SHERMAN CARTER BARNHARD
Photography: WALT ROYCRAFT

The DiLeonardo International design team was presented with the challenge to develop this "first" all-suite concept for the Hilton Inns, Inc. chain. Situated deep in the bluegrass country of Kentucky, an antebellum theme was chosen to portray the gracious accommodations and true Southern hospitality of the era before the American Civil War.

Patrician colors of deep green, blue, red and gray were combined with saddle tan for an American Empire look. The checkered lobby floor in hues of gray/blue and green enhances the rich verde green marble of the registration desk.

The dramatic six-story atrium forms the central core of this new property. From tier-glassed balcony corridors, guests can view the activity below. Trailing vines, over-scaled planted palms, lush green carpeting, and stone statuary capture the feeling of a formal Southern Garden.

Ascending to the second floor lobby, the feeling of Southern comfort and charm are equally conveyed by the unusual pairing of a dark green velvet-and-oxblood red wicker in the lounge. Scroll-footed Empire sofas upholstered in black gross point fabric, and an inset patterned carpet, reinforce the character development of this property.

In the "Polo Restaurant," wrought-iron gates, simulated stone quoin-work and statuary, complement the theme. The use of black watch plaid upholstery on banquettes teamed with tan leather-look vinyl on contemporary pull-up chairs and sandblasted silhouettes of running horses, contribute to an equestrian feeling.

In the guest suite, the parlor is equipped with a bar and under-counter refrigerator. A dressing area, closet, and bath separate the living and sleep quarters. A mahogany and beveled mirror-doored armoire, together with a carved poster headboard in the bedroom, pick up on the American Empire theme.

The registration desk provides a welcoming element for the incoming guest and sets the theme of the design—a combination of American Empire and contemporary hi-tech.

The second floor seating area exhibits the unusual pairing of dark green velvet and oxblood red wicker. Scroll-footed Empire sofas are upholstered in black gross point fabric.

Traditional mahogany furnishings are found in the guest suite. Queen Anne armchairs in plaid wool contrast well against the deep plush carpet. A jewel-toned paisley printed fabric coverlet and a tapestry ottoman accent the decor.

A raised parquet floor leads patrons into the "Chuckers Lounge." Design elements were taken directly from a tack room. Wood-framed sliding glass doors, covering the liquor display, are reminiscent of barn doors. Narrow vertical board is used on the front of the bar.

Natural brown suede fabric is used for upholstery in the parlor area of the guest suite. Distinctive brass desk lamp illuminates equestrian painting.

EMBASSY SUITES
DEERFIELD

Location: DEERFIELD, ILLINOIS, USA
Interior Design: DESIGN CONTINUUM, INC.
Architecture: SOLOMON, CORDWELL,
                  BUENZ & ASSOC.

Unusual for a suburban hotel, the contemporary tropical setting and color palette—reminiscent of an island retreat—are part of the design concept of the 237-suite Embassy Suite Hotel. "The hotel management wanted guests to feel that they are getting away from all the pressures of daily life when they check into the hotel," says Woody Faust, project designer.

Upon entering the hotel, the eye is drawn to the seven-story skylighted atrium, an aspect characteristic of most suite hotels. Glass enclosed elevators rise above the verdant setting of planting, streams, waterfalls, walkways and gazebos.

Situated in the center of the atrium is the Tropical Cafe. To enter; guests cross a bridge and a bubbling stream. The contemporary rattan and stained burgundy furniture is offset with striped upholstery. Carpeting in a rich pattern of greens, burgundy, teal, beige and soft roses completes the setting. Gazebos with faux copper gabled roofs provide covering for restaurant patrons.

The use of pools, waterfalls, and abundant foliage, provides a soothing atmosphere for the hotel guests. Subtle touches of polished and flamed granite imported from Portugal round out the lobby design.

Spacious guest suites are tastefully decorated in mint green, coral blue and accents of pale yellow. Green carpeting enhances the pickled pine furnishings. Each has a bedroom with a marble vanity, a conference/dining table, a sitting area with sofabed, a wet bar with microwave oven, refrigerator and coffee maker.

The Presidential and Governor's Suites are more lavishly appointed. Walls are covered in silk, while black lacquer furnishings exhibit an Oriental influence. Dining/conference tables were custom-made in Spain and two marble baths feature Jacuzzis.

All guest suites feature limited edition abstract contemporary lithographs by American artists.

Guests are welcomed into the Tropical Cafe through a one-and-a-half story entry arch with a faux copper roof.

A corporate atmosphere is created in the conference room through use of wood paneling and carpeting in tones of deep green and mauve. Two-tiered glass chandeliers provide additional lighting. Pastel artwork accents business-like surroundings.

Black lacquer furnishings exhibit an Oriental influence in the Presidential Suite. Carpeted floors have a marble border in the parlor with a full marble floor in the dining area. A faux copper chandelier adds soft light to the dining/conference table.

RADISSON SUITE HOTEL

Location: INDIANAPOLIS, INDIANA, USA
Hotel Company: RADISSON HOTEL CORP.
Interior Design: CSA, INC.
Architecture: RTKL DESIGN ARCHITECTS
Photography: LEA BABCOCK

It is not often that you find two sibling hotels standing adjacent to one another in one city. Such is the case, however, in Indianapolis, where both the Radisson Plaza and Radisson Suite hotels are found.

To gain a greater share of the hospitality market, Radisson management decided to add an all-suite hotel next to the four-year-old Radisson Plaza. Linking the two properties with skywalks, it was possible to have each benefit from the others' amenities.

The theme selected for the Radisson Suite Hotel was a timeless, traditional club atmosphere catering primarily to executive business travelers. This contrasts with the modern setting found in its sister hotel.

The challenge faced by designers from CSA, the in-house design group at Radisson, was to integrate the public spaces while creating warmth and humanistic qualities with large volumes of space. Using skywalks, guests could benefit from health club facilities and eating establishments, which are generally not part of the all-suite package.

The outstanding feature upon entering the hotel is the monumental 40-foot mural commissioned specifically for the loggia with a two-story colonnade. Warm, rich tones of blue, green and red against cherry and mahogany period furnishings were used to give a timeless classical appearance. Generous use of brass and marble accent the traditional decor.

One of the more interesting aspects of this 160-suite hotel are the several two-level suites which provide the ultimate in privacy. A clubhouse atmosphere continues through the parlor area located on the first floor and the sleeping quarters on the second floor. The use of rich woods and marble, offset by striped upholstery and floral fabric coverlets, create an aura of genteel comfort.

The design of the Radisson Suite Hotel creates a cozy residential environment with a well-established look.

A tromp l'oeil balustrade in the hotel's loggia gives emphasis to the massive mural surrounding a seating niche.

Dark cherry wood furnishings in the lobby add to the clublike atmosphere of the 160-suite hotel.

Period furniture in the Board Room Salon is accented by tones of colonial blue in the upholstery and carpet design. French doors insure privacy between the meeting room and parlor area.

An armoire lends definition to the seating and dining area of a typical guest suite.

Japanese watercolor on the wall and the floral fabric coverlet add an Oriental flair to this traditional bedroom.

WESTWOOD MARQUIS HOTEL & GARDENS

Location: LOS ANGELES, CALIFORNIA, USA
Interior Design: RALEIGH INTERIORS
Architecture: RALEIGH DESIGN GROUP
Photography: CHARLES S. WHITE

When presented with the task of renovating the 4-star, all-suite Westwood Marquis, designers from Raleigh Enterprises were confronted with the problem of how to best decorate the property in a distinctive California style—elegant yet easy, light yet not garish.

The plan in renovating the main lounge was to evoke the living room of a gracious residence. To accomplish this, the existing soda bar was replaced with a smaller, sleek English-style bar at the back of the room. By opening the adjacent wall, the bar could now serve guests in the Garden Room. Oriental carpets were introduced for luxurious color and pattern.

Bringing the outdoors inside was a talent that Charles T. Mayew II, the director of interiors at Raleigh Enterprises, expressed when restoring the Garden Terrace Restaurant. Although the room was originally designed to be "al fresco," it was dull and poorly lit. Windows were hidden by heavy draperies, and chairs were covered in deep burgundy. The Victorian grace of the gazebo was obscured by its surroundings. New lighting and rosebud carpeting was installed and floral tablecloths were added to enhance an outdoor, "sunny California" quality. Original lattice work was removed and replaced after backgrounds were repainted.

In the Erté Room, named after the renowned artist, Erté, a relatively small space was made to seem larger by the addition of glass cases on both sides of the entry. This substitute for windows provided an excellent opportunity to display Chinese jade trees in cloisonne pots as well as authentic reproductions of T'ang Dynasty treasures.

Upon completion of the redesign, Mayhew remarked, "If the essence of true hospitality is making guests totally at home, then the Westwood Marquis Hotel & Gardens is the perfect host."

Guests can enjoy the original alphabet prints by Erté in the Erté Room which was designed to stimulate the senses and promote conversation.

A Matisse print over the sofa in the sitting room contributes a complement of turquoise and purple to the pale peach and jade green surroundings.

The bedroom features a sumptuous half-canopied bed suitable for a Hollywood star.

The Victorian grace of the Garden Terrace was recaptured through the rejuvenation of the gazebo and addition of twig chairs to expand the seating area. An "outdoor" quality is created by the addition of floral tablecloths and rosebud carpeting.

The Westwood Lounge serves as an ideal meeting place. Chairs, representing a variety of styles, are arranged in groups of four to eight, while recessed lighting provides gentle illumination to promote comfort and relaxation.

Jill Cole

*I*n a bathroom, a lobby, a dining area, or even a corridor—will the guest know he's in a palace hotel? Yes, because "the palaces" can't quite be mistaken for anything else.

They are "great edifices designed to ensure the guest's every comfort in the most opulent style imaginable," states Jill Cole of Cole-Martinez-Curtis & Associates, Marina Del Rey, California, USA. "The guest expects not only the superlative service of a 5-star, but also a splendid structure—a classic building that has had at least 50 years to develop a patina."

What's required to accomplish the interior design of a palace is a "function of the building condition," she admits, but her enthusiasm is boundless. "The designer who has the opportunity to become involved with one of these remarkable buildings is indeed fortunate."

Cole then explains how the design process works.

"First, time must be taken to study the history of the project. The sensitive challenge is to maintain the original design intent while bringing the building up to the standards expected in today's 5-star properties. Working around the installation of heat, lighting, air-conditioning and modern plumbing can be daunting to the designer who decides to maintain the original design integrity."

The palace hotel is possessed of "much history . . . meaningful to the local community and the world at large," she warns. "Certainly the public spaces should be given careful attention because these areas . . . are responsible for giving the guest a sense of the place.

"It is a mistake to short change the guest rooms in favor of public spaces. The entire experience of a palace hotel must be splendid. Attention to detail must carry through even to the back of the house to ensure that the service will be commensurate with the appearance."

In the palace hotels, for every "upstairs" there is a "downstairs," and the opulence tends to continue even into areas generally unseen by the guest.

Palace hotels are special. They are the grande dames of the industry, the opulent queens reigning endlessly.

THE ADOLPHUS

Location: DALLAS, TEXAS, USA
Interior Design: COLE MARTINEZ CURTIS
                  & ASSOCIATES
Architecture: JERDE PARTNERSHIP INC. (DESIGN)
                  BERAN & SHELMIRE
Photography: TOSHI YOSHIMI

The Adolphus calls itself a "graceful anachronism." Historic and architecturally magnificent with its beer bottle minaret and gargoyles representing motifs of Busch brewing, the Adolphus was built by Adolphus Busch to become a queen of hotels for the king of beers.

But it has secrets only its interior designer can tell.

The interior—except for the French Room—was completely gutted back to the slabs and insides of the exterior walls. The old hotel had 850 rooms; the "new" has 436.

After research and soul-searching, the designers concluded that the old hotel wasn't "the gem" everyone thought it was, and if a pure restoration were accomplished, no one would really be pleased.

"Consequently," they admit, "we decided to create what everyone thought they remembered the hotel was like." The result is that today the Adolphus is what it was always supposed to be.

There is no true period or style in the hotel, but rather it is "mood traditional." The lobby areas are predominantly French in furnishings, while guest rooms are predominantly English.

The variety of room plans sent the designers back to their drawing boards. Every guest room floor plan was eccentric; the final solution was no less than 32 different "typical" guest room plans, and 11 different suite plans.

The renovation of the Adolphus is of extremely high quality. It has won numerous awards. The owners never compromised the design: as an example, old wood French windows were replaced with wood, although metal frames would have made no difference in the visual impact and were a fraction of the cost.

A collection of fine artists had to be found able and willing to go 16 feet into the scaffolding with the plasterers and plumbers to do the murals in the French Room.

Antique French sofa and inspiring tapestry in the wood paneled lobby are lighted by traditional lamps. Ornately carved table beneath the tapestry is highly admired.

This is "the" chandelier of the Adolphus, magnificently wrought and framed by twin staircases leading to mezzanine. Carpeting matches that of the French Room bar.

A team of expert muralists worked around and with technicians to restore the French Room, which has one of America's finest French menus.

The French Room bar is an elegant place in which to await a dining table. The black and rose floral carpeting is thematic.

PALACE HOTEL
MADRID

Location: MADRID, SPAIN
Interior Design: MUNOZ, ROSES AND NEVILLE
Architecture: AGUSTIN GOMEZ RAHOLA

Imagine the unique location of the Palace Hotel Madrid, built in 1912 by personal order of King Alphonso XIII. In the very heart of Madrid, it was luxuriously decorated with exquisite wood furnishings and rugs specially produced by the Royal Tapestry factory. Solid, lavish, majestic—one of the last hotels built in "Belle Epoque" style.

Its guests are the famous and the infamous: Nixon, Mitterand and Trudeau, Hemingway, Montand and Markevitch, Baez, Magaloff and Domingo. Even Mata-Hari.

But this great palace hotel isn't even the most famous or the most visited building on the Plaza de las Cortes: that honor belongs to its neighbor across the street, the del Prado, one of the world's most magnificent museums.

If competition brings out the best in a hotel, then the Palace Hotel Madrid competes with Goya, El Greco, and the Spanish masters.

The renovation and restoration of this beautiful building is eclectic. Its original design is supplemented with modern, and augmented by a trompe l'oeil entrance hall.

The result is sumptuous, ranging from Spanish Classic to Art Deco.

Fantastically pillared and domed inside, the massive exterior is set off in a park-like setting. The interior was redesigned while the hotel was open and operating, and it took more than six years to design the 520 rooms and public spaces.

Corinthian columns uphold the dome of the lavish lobby of the Palace Hotel Madrid, one of the last Belle Epoque-style hotels to be built.

Fireplaces and large spaces are welcoming surprises in this neo-modern guest room.

The entrance hall was redesigned as trompe l'oeil, a colorful, pleasant shock for visitors who enter after being with the Spanish masters in the del Prado across the street.

BEAU-RIVAGE
PALACE

Location: LAUSANNE, SWITZERLAND
Interior Design: GUY-MARIE KIEFFER (CAFE)
                   JEAN-CLAUDE SECOND (4th FLOOR)
Architecture: GUIDO COCCHI (CAFE)
                   (HUNZIKER & MARMIER (4th FLOOR)

On the shores of Lake Geneva is the spectacular Beau-Rivage, a palace hotel synonymous with sumptuousness and lavish service.

When "the Beau" changes a spoon, it's news: the old building was erected in 1861 and the "new" building was opened Easter Sunday of 1912, two years before Serajevo was to inaugurate the first of the "wars to end all wars."

If there's a country of peace, it's neutral Switzerland; if there's an oasis of opulent tranquility, it's the Beau-Rivage.

It was news, in the summer of 1988, when the Cafe Beau-Rivage was opened under the arcades facing the lake. Characterized by neo-classical architecture, it has a constant studied elegance and a cohesion of pilasters, moldings, alcoves and mirrors. The facade of the Cafe has large sliding bay windows which open onto a terrace decorated with Venetian blinds and lighted by bronze lamps that are replicas of those in the Palace of Versailles.

While local free-lance architect, Guido Cocchi, and the Parisian interior designer Guy-Marie Kieffer of the famed Gismondi Gallery, are winning high praise for the Cafe, the comfortable furniture, shimmering fabric and lamps were selected by the hotel's resident manager, Irmgard Muller, a touch almost expected in the grande dame hotels.

Far more rugged an undertaking was the complete renovation of the 4th (and highest) floor of the original hotel. To convert 31 rooms into 17 apartments took 27 miles of pipe and wire, 10,000 square feet of tile, and 6,000 pounds of sky blue, beige, and rose paint.

All the modern amenities are present, a far cry from 1861, but this "Bel Etage"; is furnished in Louis XVI style.

She's still the "old Beau," with her eternally unobstructed view of lake and mountain, the same old lavish service, and same old sumptuous opulence.

Furniture in neo-classic Cafe Beau-Rivage was selected by the hotel manager instead of the designer, an old European tradition.

The highest loft in the old wing is the Somerset Maugham Suite with its upper wooden balcony. It has a terrace on the roof.

The Paderewski Suite features a baby grand piano in a sumptuous room where modern styles predominate.

DON CE SAR
BEACH RESORT

Location: ST. PETERSBURG, FLORIDA, USA
Hotel Company: REGISTRY HOTEL CORPORATION
Interior Design: DESIGN CONTINUUM, INC.
Architecture: ANDERSON PARRISH ARCHITECTS
Photography: MILROY/MCALEER

The old flamingo pink hotel down at the end of the beach was crying for attention. The Don CeSar had been built in the '20s as a glamorous resort for the famous and the infamous, but it fell upon hard times.

In the '40s, the government renovated it into military offices, and then in the '50s it was renovated into a heavy, dark oak-and-wrought-iron "faux" Mediterranean style hotel.

Design Continuum was brought in to restore its pre-war elegance. There wasn't much left. Original details were gone. Few photographs remained. A historic restoration was both impossible and unwarranted.

But returned to elegance it was. French doors leading into the arcade were fashioned on a design found in old French doors stuck away in another corner of the hotel. Palladian windows approximate the originals. The rooms were small with high ceilings, so they were detailed with crown moldings. Mirrors added to the enlarged feel of bathrooms.

With such incredible exterior proportion, it's hard to believe the Don CeSar only has 277 guest rooms. All are done over in the same bright pastels and light woods found in the public spaces.

The attention to detail in this project is everywhere. This palace hotel is withstanding the test of time, looking out over the Gulf of Mexico in true Spanish/Floridian style, recapturing the youth of America's "roaring '20s" while not letting anyone see any of the troubles she faced while growing up.

The Don CeSar—an architectural delight from the Roaring '20s—shows how beautiful she is in an evening gown.

This gilt antique marble table in its floral setting is typical of the new light and airy renovation that has replaced the once dark Mediterranean style of this palace hotel.

"European eclectic" is a broad description for the blue tones, gray marbles, wooden bannisters, magnificent chandelier and draperies in the redone lobby of the Don CeSar. Its sea-and-sand palette matches its site on the Gulf of Mexico.

Magnificent chandeliers and minimalized French-style stairs bring out the scope of the windows in this portion of the Don CeSar.

PALACE LUZERN

Location: LUCERNE (LUZERN), SWITZERLAND

This huge marbled bathroom is in keeping with a hotel that surprised Lucerne with the large number of baths it provided back in 1906.

Minimalist furnishing can be spectacular, as in this private dining area where brilliant golds and bright whites are relieved only by delicate floral arrangements and the green carpet.

When the Palace Lucerne opened in 1906, it was Lucerne's first building of reinforced concrete. Elegant and highly detailed, its exterior is framed by beautiful Lake Lucerne.

But its ownership history was a difficult one. During the crisis years of the '30s, with its combination of Depression and the ominous tones of war, it ended up in the hands of a Munich speculator who terribly neglected it.

Then in the '40s it became a military first aid station and was used to store supplies and provisions for the war commissary.

But the hotel was repaired in 1945-46 and reopened on June 1, 1946, as the first entirely renovated upper-class hotel in Lucerne. It was the favorite stopping place for American GIs on leave from Germany.

Today, many of those once-young American soldiers go back to the palace hotel, the grande dame hotel with its opulent lobby, dominated by a breathtaking chandelier and complemented by elegant tapestries.

Each of the 165 guest rooms has its own unique decor. Since 1971, the hotel has been in a constant process of renovation, restoration and redesign.

Back when it first opened, it was famous for its large number of bathrooms. Today, it still seems to "specialize" in gorgeous bathrooms, pampering guests in marbled luxury.

It is very clean-lined in most public areas: the columns stress an Ionic theme rather than the ornate Corinthian style, and the terrace balconies are concrete held up by gargoyles and surrounded by wrought iron.

It is a landmark of cultured elegance.

UMAID BHAWAN
PALACE

Location: JODHPUR, INDIA
Hotel Company: WELCOMGROUP
Photography: HARDEV SINGH

Built in 1942, the Umaid Bhawan Palace was the largest private residence in the world at that time. This palace-turned-hotel is still the residence of the Maharaja of Jodhpur.

He might be hard to find: the hotel covers 3.5 acres, even though it only has 66 rooms.

Its opulence is perhaps the most awe-inspiring in the world. It took 3,000 artisans 13 years to put together this edifice of hand-chiseled sandstone blocks—an interlocking architectural triumph because it uses no mortar.

The Trophy bar is rich Burmese teak, and the lobby is crowned with an inner dome of 105 feet—with a central dome that rises 80 feet above that. Sofas are upholstered in velvet.

But was all this opulence created simply for visiting foreigners, as "just another" oasis for wealthy travelers?

Not at all. The most stirring part of the story is why it was built in the first place. in 1931 there was a terrible famine in Jodhpur. So the Maharaja decided to build his palace to employ all his people.

The rooms are lavish. One, the Maharani Suite, contains a bathtub carved out of a single piece of marble.

Covering 3.5 built-up acres on 26 acres of gardens, the Umaid Bhawan Palace was once the world's largest private residence. The Maharaja of Jodhpur still lives here.

To construct the sweeping staircases and the soaring dome, more than one million square feet of the finest marble was used.

This bathtub in the Maharani Suite is carved from a single piece of pink marble.

LA MAMOUNIA

Location: MARRAKESH, MOROCCO
Interior Design: ANDRE PACCARD

Legend has it that there has always been an olive grove and a garden in the heart of Marrakesh, below the dazzling snows of the Atlas Mountains.

So extraordinary was this garden, the Sultan Sidi Mohammad and his wife, the great Lalla Fatima, gave it to their son as a wedding present.

Then, in 1922, Prost and Marchisio decided to build "the most beautiful hotel in the world" on that spot. They may have succeeded.

Every year, Winston Churchill came here and sat on the terrace with his paints, trying to recapture the glory of the gardens and mountains. Royalty of every description vacationed in La Mamounia.

With its 179 rooms and 49 suites, it was renovated several years ago to "bring back its true soul." Once again the rooms are worthy of sleeping coaches on the Orient Express or the cabins of Normandy. There are three private villas amid the orange and olive groves.

The hotel has six restaurants and six bars, ranging from traditional Moroccan food and motif, to the highest-class French.

Robert Elegant, writer for the *New York Times*, quotes the French interior designer, Andre Paccard, as having this bold motto: "Too much is not enough."

The theme of the hotel, according to its manager, the venerable Jacques Bouriot, is "Art Deco and traditional Moroccan."

Even though some bathrooms are now glass and chrome, they still have gold-plated faucets.

Jacques Brel wrote in the guest book: "La Mamounia remains a civilized dream." Enough said!

The awesome twilight face of La Mamounia glows, surrounded by gardens some claim are the "gardens of Hesperides." The splendid, inspiring Moroccan Suite room is restored as part of what original architects tried to make "the world's most beautiful hotel."

LAUSANNE PALACE

Location: LAUSANNE, SWITZERLAND
Hotel Company: SWISSOTEL

Elegant dining in the formal style: the blue and wood motif, with the Lausanne Palace's inevitable columns and magnificent chandeliers, peacefully belie the war-torn days of the hotels inauguration.

When the Lausanne Palace opened in 1915, Europe was in the throes of terror. But it had one piece of luck: King Victor Emmanuel of Italy had waited just long enough before declaring against Emperor Franz Joseph to allow the Italian sculptors to finish their magnificent work on the facade.

Instead of opening to the doves of peace, it opened to the guns of war. The Palace was a refuge for fleeing foreigners. After work in the hotel, Swiss women would run to the train station to bring treats and flowers to the badly wounded French troops.

What a start for a palace hotel—but perhaps a good one, for these kinds of hotels are a refuge from the fears and worries of the world, offering the greatest degrees of opulence and personal service.

Grand marble staircases and intricate Corinthian columns are every-where. Carved box-chairs and elegant French-style furnishings give it almost a museum quality.

The spectacular columns in the "grand style" lobby are unmistakable, as are the suddenly-found intimate eating areas that seem to spring from nowhere.

All the 170 rooms and suites are individually appointed. The hotel was begun in 1913, but the furnishings were originally of the turn of the century style, not the then-slightly modernized versions being produced in the "era of good feeling." With exceptional perseverance and attention, the hotel has been able to preserve almost all of the original furniture and fireplaces.

This is part of what makes a palace hotel such a queen of hostelry and interior design: the tremendous expense taken to preserve, when it's many times less expensive simply to replace.

Although totally modern in its amenities, some rooms feature French-style furniture that is more than 75 years old.

MENA HOUSE
OBEROI

Location: CAIRO, EGYPT
Hotel Company: OBEROI HOTELS

Excellence, like pyramids, never goes out of style.

Mena House Oberoi should know: it is nestled among the Pyramids of Egypt, in historic Cairo. The Sphinx is literally just the other side of the hotel's golf course, as are the Step Pyramid of Zoser and the legendary Tomb of Ti.

And towering above the hotel is none other than the Great Pyramid itself.

The Mena House Oberoi has 40 acres of jasmine-scented gardens. Its furniture is arabesque, inlaid with mother of pearl. The mosaic tiles are hand-crafted. The wood doors are magnificently carved, and encased in brass. Original works of art and magnificent antiques are everywhere, as befits a palace hotel set amid one of the cradles of civilization.

Its rooms and 18 suites are sumptuous, and delicate framed windows open onto views of the Great Pyramid. The suites are among the finest in the Mediterranean. The Churchill and the Montgomery suites are masterpieces of elegance.

Everywhere are pointed arches of Arab design, delicate themes in wood, wicker or marble.

The interior design fits perfectly with this arabesque architecture, combining understated natural elegance and lavish design.

Fit for a king? Of course—the staff of the Mena House Oberoi likes to tell guests, "It's here that the Pharoahs stayed while they were building the pyramids." It isn't quite that old, but since 1869 it's been one of the world's most famous palace hotels.

For 120 years the arabesque Mena House Oberoi has graced the skyline of Cairo. Its neighbor, the Great Pyramid, has been there even longer.

The hotel's famous marble corridor leads through a succession of pointed arches. Jewel-tones glass beads cascade down this breathtaking chandelier.

CHAPTER 9

Mega Hotels

John Jones

*M*EGA—a prefix indicating something over-large, gargantuan, monumental, or mammoth in size. Those are the exact superlatives that come to mind when one envisions a "Mega Hotel." These properties are more than 1,000 rooms in size, and in some cases more than 3,000.

As John Jones, manager of creative design at FORMA, puts it, "Mega hotels are often cities within a city, containing a mind-boggling array of restaurants, lounges, shops, sports and convention facilities, business and meeting rooms, and other services that make them virtually self-sufficient. They significantly impact—and sometimes dominate— their immediate environment, if not the entire city in which they are located."

A great number of difficulties must be overcome when designing for a mega hotel. Not only must the architect design a structure that has a positive affect on its environment and surroundings, but he must also meet an array of program-matic and economic requirements.

Jones continues, "For the interior designer, there is the matter of 'humanizing' a huge, impersonal space —of imparting warmth and personality and a sense of identity while respecting the architect's scale and materials. He is also challenged with avoiding redundancy by including elements that will be delightful and memorable over time so that, no matter how many times people visit the hotel, they will always find it fresh, invigorating and special."

However, the most important design element is lighting. "It can define and differentiate spaces. It can create interest and contrast—warmth and intimacy in one space, energy and vitality in another. Lighting can also be used to encourage guests to explore their environs," notes Jones.

And what is the future trend in mega hotel design? Jones feels, "In the next five years, mega hotels will probably become even more eclectic and inter-national in character reflecting the 'shrinking' world we live in today, and the global culture that is developing. Hotel designers will be challenged to do more than merely create a rich, residen-tial aesthetic. Increasingly, we will be called upon to give hotel guests more than they experience at home."

WALDORF-ASTORIA

Location: NEW YORK, NEW YORK, USA
Hotel Company: HILTON HOTELS CORP.
Interior Design: KENNETH HURD ASSOCIATES
                        INTERIOR DESIGNS INTERNATIONAL, INC.
                        (SUITE ONLY)
Architecture: SCHULTZE & WEAVER
Photography: NATHANIEL LIEBERMAN IDI
                        (SUITE ONLY)

Whether you walk down the Silver Corridor flanked by lush palms and vaulted ceilings or enter the Park Avenue Lobby , crystal chandeliers provide a regal illumination to all aspects of the Waldorf Astoria.

There are some hotels that set a certain standard by which all others are judged. The standard bearer for "mega hotels" is the 1,600-room Waldorf-Astoria in New York City, which calls itself the first of the giants.

Originally completed in 1931, the hotel has been undergoing a massive renovation and restoration at an estimated cost of US$110,000,000. Every facet of the property is being affected. Because of the new fire laws, which stipulate the addition of sprinklers, the focal point is on the public areas rather than the guest rooms—a reversal of usual hotel design objective.

Cost has not been spared in rejuvenating this grande dame. Materials have been gathered from all over the world—Honduras, Czechoslovakia, Thailand, Hong Kong.

The Park Avenue lobby is a plethora of architectural detail in an Art Deco style. Overlooking the entrance from the Cocktail Terrace, one views stately columns of Rockwood stone executed in a modern classical style. A series of floral bouquets, superimposed on lattice work of nickel and bronze, form an ornate balustrade encircling the lobby. The focal point in this area is the imposing marble mosaic medallion called the "Wheel of Life," consisting of 148,000 separate pieces.

The 113 suites in the adjacent Waldorf Towers are also receiving a facelift. Located between the twenty-seventh and the forty-second floors, all of the guest rooms offer an awe-inspiring view of New York.

With its opulent and plush interior, the Waldorf-Astoria continues to set the standard for worldwide mega hotels. It is, therefore, no wonder that she remains the flagship of the Hilton Hotels Corp. chain.

International cultural artifacts add interest to the eclectic seating area of this suite.

The living room of this luxurious suite is richly appointed with flat marbled columns flanking a window, a marble fireplace topped with a gilded round mirror, and floral carpeting accented by plush textured upholstery.

A starburst marbled floor and a burled wood grandfather clock welcome guests into the rich red-walled foyer of this guest room. The dining area is accented with a crystal chandelier and muraled wall.

Seventeen crystal chandeliers hang over the upper boxes in the Grand Ballroom done in shades of flattering rose and off-white.

CHICAGO HILTON
AND TOWERS

Location: CHICAGO, ILLINOIS, USA
Hotel Company: HILTON HOTELS CORP.
Interior Design: HIRSCH/BEDNER & ASSOCIATES
Architecture: SOLOMON, CORDWELL,
                     BUENZ & ASSOCIATES
Photography: JAIME ARDILES-ARCE

In a time when most hotels are adding rooms, the Chicago Hilton and Towers has cut its total by half. The Stevens Hotel, as it was known in 1927 when it opened, originally had 3,000 rooms and was billed as the "largest hotel in the world." During the recent extensive renovation and restoration program, the rooms were decreased to 1,620. Many of the original rooms were converted into multi-room suites, while others were combined to enlarge existing guest rooms.

The US$185 million renovation and restoration process included gutting the entire hotel, restoring its historic and irreplaceable design elements, and adding a seven-story building for parking, exhibit space and health club facilities.

The goal of the designers at Hirsch/Bedner & Associates was to add an aura of grandeur, usually expected in small hotels, to a mammoth structure through the use of traditional architecture.

The first overwhelming aspect, as one enters the hotel, is the lobby's Great Hall. It took Lido Lippi, an Italian-born artist, seven months to hand-restore the large ceiling mural. He was suspended 36 feet above the ground on scaffolding Michaelangelo-style. A poultice was applied to the travertine marble to cleanse away 60 years of impurities, uncovering exquisite cartouches, columns and architectural detailing.

Artifacts from the luxury liner Normandie's first-class lounge, which were purchased by the hotel's previous owners, accent the Normandie Lounge, which overlooks the Great Hall. The SS Normandie sank in 1927, after a fire, in New York Harbor the year the original hotel was opened.

Every guest room and bathroom was totally renovated. A residential feeling of comfort and relaxation is promoted by the use of cherry-wood, Hepplewhite-style furnishings. Subtle tones of mauve and gray in the decor are accented by original works by Chicago artists. Italian marble floors and walls, and brass fixtures are characteristic of each bathroom. Some of the rooms are "double doubles," featuring two large beds and two complete bathrooms.

With all the varied facilities and amenities offered, this six-award winning hotel is the essence of a "city within a city"—a concept hard to imagine in Chicago.

The Board room in the Chicago Hilton is illuminated in regal splendor by crystal chandeliers and wall sconces.

The Grand Ballroom and the Great Hall exude a shear opulence reminiscent of the great palaces of Europe.

Italian marble pervades the newly renovated bathrooms, with potted plants adding a perfect contrast.

WESTIN STAMFORD & WESTIN PLAZA AT RAFFLES CITY

A very clean, no-frills design of the elevator lobby is a stark contrast to the tropical setting of the Palm Grill in the Westin Plaza.

Location:	RAFFLES CITY, SINGAPORE
Hotel Company:	WESTIN HOTELS & RESORTS
Interior Design:	FORMA
Architecture:	I.M. PEI & PARTNERS
Photography:	EDEN ARTS

What does Singapore have that can be found nowhere else on the globe?—The world's tallest hotel, the 73-story Westin Stamford! In fact, there are two Westin hotels in this office complex located in Raffles City. The other is the 28-story Westin Plaza, and together the two properties offer 2,053 rooms.

According to John Jones, manager of creative design at FORMA, "We based our design on an overall concept of harmony and contrast. In the larger-scaled, public spaces where Pei's architectural statement is strongest, we used interior elements to work with and support the grand scale and pristine use of materials. In smaller, architecturally independent spaces, contrasts and counterpoints were created to the overall Pei design."

As would be expected in a Far East setting, furnishings are spare and contemporary. Guest rooms were created to be refreshing departures from the humid, tropical outdoor environment. Jones continues, "Each guest room needed to be a welcome 'oasis' in the midst of a giant hotel complex and a huge, bustling city." Soothing color tones of natural beige contrasting with rich green, as well as marble tabletops in bathrooms and entryways, were chosen to convey coolness and comfort.

Lighting, as in all mega hotels, played an important role. An example of this is Somerset's Bar in the Westin Plaza. "We were challenged to create a warm and romantic gathering place to contrast dramatically with the contemporary, architectural exterior. Smaller apertures and lower voltages were used to diminish the expanse of the room and create intimacy," says Jones.

With all the careful, meticulous planning that went into designing both the exteriors and interiors of this giant complex, it is no wonder it took six years to complete.

Situated atop the world's tallest hotel, the expansive spaces of the Compass Rose restaurant are reduced with innovative lighting, both natural and artificial.

One can witness a spectacular view of Singapore's harbor from one of the Compass Rose dining areas.

Somerset's Bar offers a gathering place rich in texture and character.

The side pavilion of the Compass Rose is enclosed by large marble columns. Color tones of lavender and rose add warmth to this spacious room.

The geometric design of the black and beige marble floor add accent to the terra-cotta colored surrounding of the women's restroom.

The Empire Room, that premiere supper club with its elegant white glove service, has been restored to its original 1925 magnificence in eye-boggling gold and green, lorded over by its magnificent chandeliers.

PALMER HOUSE

Location: CHICAGO, ILLINOIS, USA
Hotel Company: HILTON HOTELS CORP.
Interior Design: MARK CHRISTY & ASSOCIATES

The Palmer House—is it a grand hotel, a 117-year-old historic building, or a mega? Even with 1,750 rooms, it defies categorization.

One entrance nestles quietly underneath those elevated tracks whose circular route encloses what is thusly called Chicago's "Loop." The other entrance dashingly fronts on State Street, that "great street," the life-breath of the City of Broad Shoulders.

Even the designer admits the Palmer House admits of no particular niche: he calls; it "renovation, restoration, palace hotel, grande dame and Mega hotel."

It's all these, and more. Areas of the hotel were completely closed down to minimize service disruption during the renovation. And the theme was to maintain the historical decor, which is "turn-of-the-century Old World."

Among the first projects was the restoration of the fabulous Empire Room, opened in 1925. It is one of the world's premiere supper clubs, as generations of Chicagoans and world travelers came to hear Veloz and Yolanda, Jimmy Durante, Jack Benny, Hildegarde, Maurice Chevalier, Tony Bennett and Carol Channing.

Many years of slapdash remodelings were righted, so the historic room could be reopened in its original splendor with its white glove French service. The famous chandeliers still glitter in the room of green and gold.

When the entire hotel is completed in 1989, it will have been renovated at a cost of approximately US$100 million.

The rooms are "residential palatial," with custom-made cherrywood armoires, marble-topped gaming tables, and all new furniture, wallcoverings, plumbing and bathrooms.

Once again splendidly exciting is the famous Palmer House lobby, one floor up from the street-level arcade. The magnificent ceiling mural, a composite of 21 paintings by the French artist Louis Rigal, was painstakingly restored by Lido Lippi, master restorer of Chicago's Florence Art Conservation center.

Famous lobby of the Palmer
House with its ceiling mural
and marble staircase leading
to the equally famous Empire
Room. Refurbishment includes
a classic French pouf, perfect
for people watching, flanked
by English and French
antiques of the mid-Victorian
era. The grand piano is
accompanied by a harp and
violin.

THE WESTIN HOTEL, RENAISSANCE CENTER

Location:	DETROIT, MICHIGAN, USA
Hotel Company:	WESTIN HOTELS & RESORTS
Interior Design:	FORMA
Architecture:	JAMES P. RYAN AND ASSOCIATES
Photography:	KEN PAUL

Originally designed by John Portman in 1972, the Renaissance Center's "raison d'etre" was to function as one environment, with office towers interfaced with the hotel and retail structures and all meshed together by a large, ground-level atrium.

In renovating the lobby of the 1,400-room hotel, designers at FORMA were challenged with giving the property its own identity apart from the rest of the complex. FORMA was charged with developing a design that would make a strong aesthetic statement, yet function efficiently while responding to the operational needs of such a large business and convention hotel.

The other problem presented was to accomplish all this while allowing traffic to flow conveniently and efficiently through the lobby space.

The design solution was the creation of a glass-enclosed, colonnade-style space which would separate the hotel from the rest of the Renaissance Center. The new lobby, embraced in twin rows of pillars, leads from the property's Carriage entrance, past the registration desk to the guest elevators.

Color and materials played a large part in adding warmth and rich detail to an open and non-detailed space. Because of the large amount of concrete in the center, a golden color was selected for the lobby. In addition, hand-picked Brazilian granite, which was cut in Italy, was chosen for its warmth in coloration.

Gold tones were also used not only in the custom-designed field carpeting, but also the wall fabric and upholstery. Brass finishes also added a golden touch.

Classical furniture with detailed case pieces were chosen to support the formality of the colonnade and coffered ceilings.

The design intent and solution accomplished its goal—to add definition and character to one of Detroit's premier hotels.

Lush foliage provides a splash of color to the lobby of the Westin Hotel.

Gold tones in carpeting, upholstery and brass finishes add warmth to a cold, concrete environment.

Wall sconces reflecting off the marble-tiled walls illuminate the elevator corridor.

CHAPTER **10**

Resorts

Sarah Tomerlin Lee   Linda Selzer

"*T*he basic difference between hotel design and resort design is the realization that a hotel is often an intermediate stop, while a resort is a destination," says Sarah Tomerlin Lee, president of New York-based Tom Lee Ltd.

Aptly put. Precisely because it is a "destination," a resort attracts guests who stay longer and will explore more areas of the hotel. That means that from the lobby to the dining room, and from the corridor to the swimming pool, all design elements must be eloquent and consistent.

Adding to the challenge of resort design is the fact that idyllic settings often lie in difficult climates—harsh winters or humid summers. Says Linda Selzer, vice president of Xanadu Design, with offices in the USA and Caribbean: "For hot weather resorts, we have to create interiors that are cool and refreshing as a balance to the heat and humidity outside. We try to achieve an uncluttered, spacious feeling with crisp cottons and linens, and natuiral light-colored woods. Outdoor furnishings have to dry quickly. Woods must be termite-resistant. In some areas, there are no dry cleaning facilites so all fabrics—even rugs—must be washable."

Winter resorts are no less demanding. Dark colors and more substantial furnishings must be used to create a feeling of warmth. In addition, they must withstand winter's dryness and prevent snow, tracked in with shoes and skis, from spreading a gray film throughout the property.

For the most part, these designers agree that guest rooms should be bigger and more luxurious, with particular attention paid to the bath area. "Bathrooms should be large—somewhat fantasy-like. They should have high quality fittings and use materials such as tile or marble. Also, the guest does more settling in and needs plenty of storage space, as well as a comfortable and well-lighted reading area," states Selzer.

Styles of resort are as varied as the properties themselves, taking inspiration from ancient room to avant-garde contemporary. What they share is a common purpose of enveloping guests with a relaxed feel that transports them beyond everyday life.

ELDORADO HOTEL

Location: SANTA FE, NEW MEXICO, USA
Hotel Company: AIRCOA
Interior Design: BARBARA ELLIOTT INTERIORS

Santa Fe is one of the few cities in the world where the phrase "city center resort" is not a contradiction in terms. Part cultural oasis, part business haven, it is as attractive to art- and sun-worshipping tourists as it is to corporate executives and conventioneers.

Designers with Barbara Elliott Interiors, based in California, had to develop a style for Santa Fe's Eldorado Hotel that would appeal to both types of guests. They decided to carry the identity of the city into the hotel, using a design idiom that focused on colors and materials native to the American Southwest.

Tiles and timbers shape much of the design in the public spaces. Accents, rather than accessories, add points of visual interest that keep "spare" from become "austere." In many of the main level corridors, potted cacti form a surreal colonnade against beige walls, interrupted by bittersweet and green stripes framing an inset of geometrically Pueblo design.

Lighting also was a key consideration. "We wanted the interiors to exude the impression of being grand and glowing. To accomplish that we used a careful mixture of natural and extra-ordinary custom lighting. We also paid close attention to the creation of architectural detailing," says Barbara Elliott.

To create sufficient but even illumination, the designers interspersed necessary indirect lighting within the architectural detailing—in some cases, worked into the mouldings, in others installed under archways. This insures even background lighting that is "highlighted" by Spanish-inspired lantern chandeliers and a variety of wall sconces.

The elegantly carved beams and rustic chandeliers that would have fit with a New World Spanish hacienda, contrast with—yet complement—the goemetric precision of the Amerind-inspired architecture details which define the doorway and elevators.

Spectacular art and artifacts serve as the design focal points for the entry to the Old House restaurant built on the site of historical adobe building, called Eldorado, once used as a rooming house.

Deep turquoise and sand beige bring the Southwestern sand and sky inside in the Old House restaurant. Carrying through the theme are natural accents: an adobe fireplace and the rustic ceiling beams.

Custom-designed seating gives a distinctive look for the Court restaurant, as does the jewel-toned tiles of the table tops.

To insure the interior styling of Eldorado would encompass a complete environment, every area was "designed"— including this corridor dramatized by a natural colonnade of potted cacti.

Natural wooden casegoods, accented by simple pulls, imbue the guest rooms with a timeless elegance appropriate for an upscale resort.

The rustic sophistication of the public spaces is translated in a consistent but softer tone for the hotel's suites. A clustering of art and artifacts around the fireplace—some of museum quality—enhances the residential mood.

The natural beauty of the timbered four-poster and lamp in this suite are played up against the plushness of the seating and the rich sunset color scheme of turquoise and rose.

DORAL SATURNIA

Location: MIAMI, FLORIDA, USA
Hotel Company: DORAL HOTELS
Interior Design: TOM LEE LTD.
Architecture: JUNG/BRANNEN ASSOCIATES
Photography: DAN FORER

Florida's Doral Saturnia is a luxurious Italian-style spa with an American accent.

Though inspired by the Tuscan spa Terme di Saturnia, dedicated to maximizing both health and beauty, this 48-suite property shows influences of health hydros from the days of the caesars to 18th Century spa-palaces.

The central building of the Doral Saturnia is clad in Tufa (fossil stone). The great mural that rims the central skylight brings to mind the fluid beauty of Boticelli's Primavera and Birth of Venus. Busts of Roman emperors reign over a corridor pierced by Palladian windows.

However, the design also stretches into a modern interpretation of these themes, sparked with occasional Art Deco or Art Nouveau. The entertainment units in the guest suites are styled like small, classic temples. Motifs used in 1st Century Rome are updated and translated into designs for etched glass panels that screen off the restaurant from the swimming pool.

Although the hotel's central staircase reflects the grandeur of Italy from imperial Rome through the Renaissance, it was created by Emile-Jacques Ruhlmann in the early 1920s for Bon Marche, the Parisian department store. Located by Sarah Tomerlin Lee, head of New York City-based Tom Lee Ltd., this exquisite example of Art Nouveau design traverses three floors of the hotel.

The US$500 thousand necessary to purchase and install this Emile-Jacques Ruhlmann Art Nouveau staircase was a worthwhile investment in design terms. With its bronze panels, it produces an aura of priceless elegance as it wends through three levels of the hotel.

Faux leopard chairs, some with arms, some without, provide black-and-white drama appropriate for the backdrop of architectural curves and columns.

Spa guests are reminded to eat light but right in this vibrant, not-so-still-life mural by British artist Elsbeth Juda.

Wall panels based on Boticelli's Birth of Venus and Primavera virtually could be logos for the Doral Saturnia which emphasizes maximized health and beauty.

A step-up sleeping chamber is
separated from the living
area of this suite by the
gentle sweep of curtain in soft
pastels.

Acclaimed interior artist Dennis Abbe created these arched, etched glass panels that stand between a dining area and the swimming pool.

Brightened by a skylight, the exercise pool needs no ornamentation other than the fossil stone walls and strategic greenery.

WELCOMGROUP MUGHAL SHERATON

Location: TAJUANG AGRA, INDIA
Hotel Company: WELCOMGROUP/
                    SHERATON CORP.
Interior Design: RAMESH KHOSLA
Architecture: ARCOP CANADA
Photography: HARDEV SINGH

Unlike beach resorts that are retreats away from civilization, the Welcomgroup Mughal Sheraton is enveloped in civilization.

It stands in Agra, a city of splendid tombs and the monument most synonymous with India—the Taj Mahal. Working in this setting, the hotel's architects and designers had little choice but to create a hotel that could hold its own against some of the artistic wonders of the world. They succeeded to such an extent that the hotel earned

the prestigious Aga Khan Award for Architecture.

The lobby and connecting corridors are faced with marble, the symbol of the Mughal lifestyle. The legend of prominent Mughals and their noblemen is played out over the portals of the hotel. There is also a marble replica of the Taj Mahal (to scale) in the lobby, for those who wish to study the building in detail.

However, the visual anchor for the lobby is a massive chandelier, claimed

to be the largest and brightest of any in the country. Glass-paneled bridges named after three queens of Akbar carry guests from the central area to the guest room wings.

In the Mughal style rooms, the ambience is ethnically correct from the bamboo blinds to the low lines of the beds and marble seats. Most of the rooms offer a traditional divan, lined with bolsters, as well as conventional seating.

Generous use of water and foliage, typical of the Mughal era, are important stylistic elements for this resort hotel. Its swimming pool is converted into an elegant party venue with formally-set tables and a halo of twinkling lights.

The opulent lifestyle of the Mughal era is translated into this guest room which features a breathtakingly intricate canopy over the beds, elegant artwork, and the traditional lounge seating enhanced by a soothing bolster.

JEKYLL ISLAND CLUB

Location: JEKYLL ISLAND, GEORGIA, USA
Hotel Company: RADISSON HOTELS CORP.
Interior Design: DESIGN SOLUTIONS/
CONCEPT SOLUTIONS
Architecture: CIRCLE DEVELOPMENT CORP.
Photography: VANN JONES MARTIN

America's "royalty" considered Jekyll Island their playground from 1887 to 1942. Though designers did not seek to recreate every aspect of that era, they wanted to recapture its posh spirit in the "rehabilitation" of the Jekyll Island Club.

Although the influence of the Victorian Age is strongly seen in the grand staircase, porte cochere and the ornate interior moldings, designer J. Linden (Buddy) McDowell, of Georgia-based Design Solutions, says "The interiors of the club are not a reproduction of the Victorian feel of 1887. Rather, they are an updated adaptation for today's guests." And all had to be done within the context of an island setting.

In the Federal Reserve Room, the color scheme flows from an original stained glass window in yellows and greens. The room itself features pale yellow as its dominate color, matched in tone by pickled pine furnishings. The adjoining J.P. Morgan room, which can be used with the Federal Reserve Room for large functions, extends this color theme. The palette deepens to terra cotta in the nearby Alexander meeting room. Soft peaches and yellows brighten most of the guest rooms.

Furnishings throughout the club were selected with an eye toward authentic lines. Simple, classic styles—primarily Queen Anne and Chippendale—complement the historic character of the building. Period gaslight fixtures were electrified and reconditioned to add special interest, along with selected artworks reminiscent of Victorian pieces.

Natural light and the refreshing white ceiling create a radiant framework for the rich wood of the floor and dining chairs used in the Riverview Lounge. The cobalt and rose color scheme was inspired by the hotel's original china.

Window seats in the lounge overlook the veranda furnished with Victorian-styled wicker rockers, tables and chairs.

Old photographs taken by some of the club's founding members sparked certain elements of design. The namesake trophy of the Boar's Head lounge hangs in the exact location as its forerunner of 1887.

Shutters were used as the guest room window treatments to enhance the cream white architectural moldings millwork, as well as to control sunlight.

An exquisite stained glass panel sets the color scheme for the Treaty Room. The lovely oval table and classic chandeliers hold the focus in the middle of the space.

A peaches and cream color scheme softens the formality of the graceful colonnade that subdivides the space. Both the columns and the carpet pattern focus all eyes on the welcoming fire.

MALLIOUHANA
HOTEL

Location: MAID'S BAY, ANGUILLA,
                BRITISH VIRGIN ISLANDS
Interior Design: PEABODY INTERNATIONAL
Architecture: PEABODY INTERNATIONAL
Photography: HEDRICH BLESSING

The tropical splendor of the interiors designed for the Malliouhana Hotel seems the only sensible choice for this 50-unit property set on the idyllic island of Anguilla. But, it took nearly two years of research before this aesthetic assumption became a reality.

Pre-planning was essential to every aspect of the design, according to Lawrence Peabody, the New York-based designer chosen by hotel owner Leon Roydon to create his "dream hotel." Although some preliminary plans had been drawn, Peabody was asked to step in and do the architecture, interiors, product design, art and landscaping for the project.

Peabody and Roydon decided to test the design before installing it full-scale. The designer developed interiors for two working prototype villas. For two years, owner and designer gauged the reaction of friends who stayed at the resort. One of the major decisions, based on guests' reactions, was to use wood-slatted windows typical of the tropics rather than homogenized sliding glass windows. Ceiling fans, too, won high marks from the guests, although supplemental air-conditioning is available.

"The intention was to incorporate visual aesthetics into pragmatically-conceived facilities, and to offer luxury and comfort amidst beautiful surrounding," notes Peabody. "That's why we were happy with the acceptance of the floor-to-ceiling jalousie windows and ceiling fans. Rattan furnishings and accessories also helped to maintain the tropical ambience and, at the same time, weather the element."

Balconied rooms bring this panoramic view inside the Malliouhana Hotel, which sits on 30 acres of the quiet island of Anguilla.

Undulating arches lend a stateliness to the entry of the hotel, while a reflecting pool, edged with poinsettias, suggests the serenity apparent in both public spaces and guest rooms.

A stunning view of the sea sky are the real design focus of the terrace dining room shown. The design is purposefully understated, stressing natural materials such as wood, rattan and tile, and natural linen colors.

White tile floors and distinctive rattan furnishings bring a tropical ambience to the guest rooms. The durability and easy maintenance of these materials ensures they will retain their good looks despite the climate.

A perfect accent for an island "dream hotel" is the almost surreal menagerie depicted in the wall panels. Evocative of French painter Henri Rousseau, these artworks add vibrant color and a thought-provoking focus to the public space.

Themes common throughout the hotel—the ceiling fan and pristine white—stylistically integrate the balconies into the body of the hotel and help blur the dividing line between interior and exterior space.

Even the wine cellar is not an afterthought. Its arched doorway reflects the graceful curves of the lobby and porte cochere.

GRAND HOTEL
ZELL AM SEE

Location: ZELL AM SEE, AUSTRIA
Hotel Company: MÖVENPICK
Interior Design: GUNTHER GRUBER
Architecture: GUNTHER GRUBER

An impressive, Classic-style building sits quietly on the peninsula that juts out into Lake Zell, framed by the morning sun reflecting off the snows of the Austrian Alps.

It is the Grand Hotel Zell am See, now run by Movenpick (which has a marketing affiliation with U.S.-based Radisson).

This Alpine resort is where one would expect to see the Franz Klammers and Jean-Claude Killys at the check-in desk, skis slung carelessly over their shoulders, waiting for a room in which to toss their bags before attacking the famed runs of the Pinzgau region.

With 66 rooms and suites (totaling 228 beds), the Grand Hotel Zell am See offers far more than simply suites with fireplaces and private saunas. When winter skiers or summer watersport and hiking enthusiasts want time for themselves, the hotel offers a trained staff to take care of children in its own kindergarten.

With a private beach and glorious terrace overlooking Lake Zell, it would be Alpine enough even without the 27-hole golf course.

One of the more beautiful design features is an interior circular function room, supported by columns, with a capacity of 200. It is equipped with the most sophisticated technical facilities for conferences and celebrations, and can be divided off with partition walls to create as many as seven different rooms.

Almost all the public spaces are quietly understated in wood and white, with elegant stairways and wooden furniture.

With its magnificent location and lovely design, the Grand Hotel Zell am See is a year-around resort not only for the athletic or the pampered, but for meetings and conventions.

The stirring Austrian Alps reflect sunlight behind the Grand Hotel Zell am See, while Lake Zell awaits skaters and the Alps skiers.

Classical columns support a
honey-combed canopy over
the curved design of the pool.
This elegant indoor pool offers
a full view of the out-of-doors.

INN OF THE SIX MOUNTAINS

Location: KILLINGTON, VERMONT, USA
Interior Design: XANADU DESIGN, LTD.
Architecture: WILLIAM MACLAY ARCHITECTS & PLANNERS
Photography: PETER ADAM (BAR, GUEST ROOM, POOL)
                 ESTO PHOTOGRAPHICS (FIREPLACE)

In the winter, guests can ski the 100 trails of Killington with its long ski season—November to June. Then in summer there is tennis, golf, water sports and hiking on the famous Appalachian Trail.

But there is another season at The Inn of the Six Mountains, a season peculiar to Americans.

It's the autumn, when people go to New England just to watch the trees change color. And the farther and more rural they can go, the more impressive and renewing is that sight.

Xanadu Design did not a mighty pleasure dome decree. It designed an interior for the 104-room resort in the Green Mountains appropriate to year-round use, and worked to avoid the hackneyed New England theme without eliminating it entirely.

The furnishings and color palette had to be totally consistent with nature, yet comfortable and elegant with a seasonal look.

Expected Colonial pieces were avoided. An eclectic feeling was created by mixing traditional shapes and colors with newer interpretations, just as visitors at different times of the year have different interpretations of the Green Mountains.

The designer admits to this: "The scale of the building is very reminiscent of the Grand Resort hotels built in the United States in the early part of this century," and explains, ". . . we wanted to pick up on that feeling by incorporating it into the marketing of the hotel."

Wooden beams in the ceiling add to the earth-tone elegance of this bar, with its upholstered "stools" that aren't stools at all, but simply long-legged chairs.

This dramatic stone fireplace is framed by wooden beamed 12x12s, drying out skiers, swimmers and nature lovers who flock to New England.

This elegant suite bedroom
highlighted by floral prints,
brings the out-of-doors inside
via a huge terrace
overlooking the forest.

The wonderful rectangular
shapes in this swimming pool
are startlingly emphasized by
simple square columns.

WESTIN MAUI

Location: MAUI, HAWAII
Hotel Company: WESTIN HOTELS & RESORTS
Interior Design: HIRSCH/BEDNER & ASSOCIATES
Architecture: LAWTON & UMEMURA
Photography: MILROY/MCALEER

"Our goal in Maui was to create interiors of simple elegance which would serve as a backdrop for the intensely beautiful island," Hirsch/Bedner's project designer, Terry Henriksen, says of the Westin Maui. He then concluded, "We also wanted to instill an ambience of playful fantasy."

Henrikson succeeded with the simple elegance, but it was senior partner Howard Hirsch, who found a kindred spirit in Christopher Hemmeter, owner and developer of the property, and created the "fantasy."

Together they took a spectacular odyssey that resulted in a spectacular feature of the hotel's design. They traveled to Hong Kong, China, Bangkok and Indonesia—to buy an art collection worth several million dollars.

The museum quality art is interspersed playfully among the landscaped areas, as well as in the lobbies, restaurants, and guest suites themselves.

The lobby is small and intimate, with natural Arizona flagstone floors, coffered ceilings, custom chandeliers, and bleached ash.

Guest suites are elegantly appointed with silk spreads and draperies. To take advantage of the beachside views, the suites include raised marble tubs.

All this art, and elegance, has created an intimacy that belies the 761 rooms (which include 28 suites and the 37-room Royal Beach Club).

The Westin Maui is a work of art with works of art, as is proper on one of the most beautiful islands in the world.

A magnificent marble bathtub is raised to view the out-of-doors through a facing window in this magnificent suite bathroom, large enough and elegant enough to be the lobby of a small hotel.

Dining on the water in the Sound of the Falls restaurant continues the design theme of combining indoors and outdoors. A water buffalo statue is part of the multi-million dollar art collection interspersed throughout Westin Maui.

The traditional elegance of wood and white, beneath the high octagonal skylight, lets Villa restaurant guests dine with Maui's swaying palms.

MARRIOTT BAY POINT RESORT

Location:	PANAMA CITY, FLORIDA, USA
Hotel Company:	MARRIOTT CORP.
Interior Design:	VHA, INC.
Architecture:	COOPER CARRY & ASSOCIATES

"Old world character" is not a design theme synonymous with Floridian resorts. Perhaps that's why it worked so well for the Marriott Bay Point Resort near Panama City.

We felt it was important to make the hotel's interiors reflect the resort's northern Gulf Coast location. Here, there are more pine trees than palm trees. A 'Palm Beach' look simply is not appropriate here," explains Victor Huff, of Denver-based design firm VHA, Inc. (formerly Victor Huff & Associates).

The result recalls the gracious elegance of a Southern plantation rather than the breezy chic of a tropical getaway. The lobby lounge, called Magnolia Court, features 20-foot silk magnolia trees. This multi-functional space offers over-stuffed armchairs for guests who want to enjoy the warmth of a limestone fireplace, or seating that permits a view of the waterfront.

Polished limestone, quarried along the rim of the Gulf Coast, also was used as the lobby flooring. The walls are played up with an antique glaze to give the look of antique parchment. To add a note of warmth into this softly reflective setting, the designer chose upholstery fabrics in warm colors such as cinnabar and yellow, sparked with splashes of tropical blues and greens. This tropical motif is emphasized mostly in accents—bright paintings and ceramics; it is the traditional flavor of the design which dominates.

Since a high-energy lounge would have been out of character in this traditional environment, the designers used rich wood furnishings and brass trims to set the tone of "a comfortable watering hole where a roaming cocktail party atmosphere pervades." Square social bars invite mingling and conversation. U-shaped sofas were positioned on 10-inch platforms so that those seated could talk with those standing and still retain eye contact.

A skilled artisan from Vancouver was called in to create the parchment look of the lobby's antique glazed walls. The floors are polished limestone quarried in the area. Only bright red poinsettias and graceful sculptures are needed to complete this picture of traditional elegance.

Handpainted ceramic tiles frame the dining room's fireplace, which climbs two stories toward the cathedral ceiling. The oak trim of the chimney is repeated in the bookcases for added residential appeal.

The gift shop conveys the thoroughness of design, reflecting the same traditional lines and colors as the other areas of this 200-room hotel.

Since the double-bay hospitality suite must be used for cocktail parties as well as executive board meetings and private dinners, its design had to be flexible. Plush seating was kept low and rounded, while table seating is high-backed and formal. Cinnabar and black, played off taupe or cream, unify the space.

Various shades of green convey the theme of the Emerald Suite which contains casegoods in warm, polished woods and a magnificent wood-canopied bed.

THE SAGAMORE

Location:	BOLTON LANDING, NEW YORK, USA
Hotel Company:	OMNI HOTELS
Interior Design:	DAROFF DESIGN INC.
Architecture:	ALESKER REIFF & DUNDON INC.
Photography:	PAUL WARCHOL

Opened in 1883 by four Philadelphia millionaires who wanted to create an exclusive resort on a 70-acre island in Lake George, Sagamore became the social center for the super-rich who had built their cottages along the lake. However, its fortunes changed. Damaged twice by fire and more by its lack of appeal to the modernists of the late 1960s and 1970s, it was closed in 1981—though not for long.

Later that year, it was sold and a massive restoration began. Interiors were gutted and rebuilt with a U.S.$65 million budget. Salvageable millwork and other historically important pieces were saved; others were reproduced.

Seventy-two paint colors were used in this 100-room property, and were carefully coordinated to create a "peaceful, easy-going mood" that would integrate all areas of the hotel. Beds and bathtubs were raised above standard heights to evoke images of the past. Elements of Neo-colonial, American Country and Adirondack styles were used throughout the hotel and its 250 new cottages.

Rooms and suites vary in size, shape and decor but many feature such traditional furnishings as Queen Anne chairs and four-poster beds.

"We wanted to give the Sagamore a design spirit that would be reminiscent of another era when furnishings were collected over a long period of time," comments Karen Daroff, principal of Philadelphia-based Daroff Design.

The rustic ceiling beams, stone fireplace and wrought iron chandeliers work with a palette of earth tones to create a relaxed atmosphere in this dining room.

A white wicker towel stand and pedestal sink with porcelain faucet knobs are perfect period reminders of the late 1880s. More subtle is the fact that the guest bathtubs are raised above modern standard heights to lend a thoughtful note of authenticity.

Restored to its original glory, Sagamore attracts both tourists and conferees to its serene setting on a 70-acre island in Lake George.

The Veranda allows guests to step back into the era when the Sagamore was a playground for Philadelphia's millionaires. Its white columns, potted palms and celadon wicker furnishings recall the hotel's Victorian origins.

FOUR SEASONS LAS COLINAS INN & CONFERENCE CENTER

Location: IRVING, TEXAS
Hotel Company: FOUR SEASONS HOTELS LTD.
Interior Design: WILSON & ASSOCIATES
Architecture: HARWOOD K. SMITH PARTNERS
Photography: JAIME ARDILES-ARCE

Bringing a sense of history to new construction was important in the design theme of the Four Seasons in suburban Dallas. Not only would this lend a sense of traditional comfort to the 315-room hotel, it would also provide visual continuity with the nearby Tournament Players Golf Course.

Arched windows in the lobby and lounge open onto views of this famous golf course. Furnishings that are tasteful but eclectic, underscore the informal elegance of the resort setting. However,

the details are definitely upscale, from the deco-style custom chandeliers framed by a coffered lobby ceiling, to the custom inset, hand-woven rugs surrounded by breccia pernice marble. Even the elevator lobby and corridors connecting the lobby with the restaurants make design statements. They showcase impressive antique artifacts and feature seating "vignettes" with tapestry chairs.

Though the hotel's golf and spa facilities make it a true resort, it also

attracts conventions. Designer Trisha Wilson, head of Dallas-based Wilson & Associates, found no dichotomy in this diverse clientele. She points out that both business and leisure travelers require a luxurious guest room where they can relax at the end of the day.

To meet these demands, each guest room has a desk, custom-designed armoire housing the television and storage space, and a lounge chair.

Design of the hotel's 26 conference rooms departs from the traditional elegance of public spaces and guest rooms in favor of a slick and contemporary look with slight touches of an American Southwestern accent.

The upper level of the Cafe
on the Green features a mix
of cheery checks and rows of
beautiful plates displayed as
art to achieve a highly
residential look.

The checkered pattern used
on the upholstered seating
serves as a charming
backdrop to the cafe's
arched entry.

Black marble and soft taupe make this guest bathroom beautiful, but its layout makes it luxurious. Its ample space provides for an ample vanity, well-lighted for make-up or shaving, as well as a separate bath and shower.

Dimmable recessed lighting and an ample screen provide necessary technology for high level meetings.

Hunting theme artwork procured in Europe, and an assortment of trophies, underscore the club atmosphere of the Game Bar.

NANTUCKET INN
RESORT

Location: NANTUCKET, MASSACHUSETTS, USA
Hotel Company: KOALA INNS OF AMERICA
Interior Design: DILEONARDO INTERNATIONAL, INC.
Architecture: RAMON H. HOVSEPIAN ASSOCIATES, INC.
Photography: WARREN JAGGER PHOTOGRAPHY, INC.

A designer who becomes part of history is rare, yet that might have happened on historic Nantucket Island as the Nantucket Inn Resort may be the last structure ever allowed to be built there.

Quaint and charming, Nantucket Island has a town council over-whelmingly strident in maintaining the picturesque environment. The building's facade had to be legally approved, so the designer went one better: he carried the flavor of the island into the entrance, lobby, reception area and bar.

The restaurant is located atop the ballastered staircase, and because it offers diners the most spectacular view of the island, its walls were lined with French doors leading on to terraces.

Simplicity of style, material and furniture were DiLeonardo's design keys. The interior palette is neutral, with strong accent paints (rich tones of red and violet blue): the woods are natural or gray-stained.

The heritage of the whaling island is found in the wicker chairs, decorative screens, and pickwood scotting. The result is uncluttered spaces.

Flowing throughout these areas are black wrought iron, purple slate, tweed carpeting and plank wood flooring. There are wormy chestnut wooden wall coverings emphasizing important areas.

The personality of the guest rooms and cottages of the 100-room inn is obtained by purposely "mismatched" collections of bedroom and sitting room furniture, such as would be obtained by a sailing culture.

A comfortable environment for guests, yes; and it all accomplished DiLeonardo's goal: "...to make this property settle quietly into the community."

The design of wooden plank floor, combining "squares" that alternate from the horizontal to the diagonal, adds to the spaciousness of the Nantucket-style lobby with its wormy chestnut, wooden walls and floral accents.

An eclectic furniture mix begins with a beautifully delicate white French wrought iron bedstead, and continues through typically New England-style wooden shutters and plank floors covered with elegant floral printed area rugs.

THE NEWPORTER RESORT

Location: NEWPORT BEACH, CALIFORNIA, USA
Interior Design: COLE MARTINEZ CURTIS & ASSOCIATES
Architecture: LANDAU PARTNERSHIP, INC.
Photography: TOSHI YOSHIMI

Even in sunny California, nothing is forever. The Newporter Resort, a multiplicity of buildings with 410 rooms, was renovated—and nothing on the interior was left untouched as a new environment was created. Additionally, the hotel stayed open during every minute of the award-winning design work.

Almost all the fixtures, furnishings and finishes were replaced: the out-of-date warm color palette was superceded by the cool pastels of seafoam green, apricot, lavender, and teal blue—colors reminiscent of the sea, sand, and sunsets over the Pacific Ocean.

Many structural changes were made, usually to bring in more sunlight and afford guests a view of the newly landscaped 26 acres that were worked out to be as casual for the short-wearing bather as they are elegant for the suit-wearing businessman.

Natural materials—rattan, terra cotta, tile, light woods and wrought iron—were blended with durable natural fabrics, cottons and wools. To bring the sunlight into the new lobby, the rear wall was converted into a series of arched French doors.

In the guest rooms, the pastel palette (with seafoam green and apricot predominating), continues the new theme of the public areas. Smaller rooms were furnished to be comfortable for a family weekend, but still allow a business traveler space to sit down with a briefcase and papers.

There are startling features: the hunter green, masculine approach is used in Duke's, the nightclub with a theme of a Western, John Wayne-style saloon. It features burgundy colored woods in the bars, stools, and tables.

The designer credits much of the success of the renovation to "...paying careful attention to the needs of the resort's primary users."

This quietly bubbling lobby fountain is framed by terra cotta-tiled floorings and custom-designed, handmade Chinese area rugs.

A modern guest room, punctuated by greenery over the door, repeats the pastel palette of the resort's public areas.

A greenhouse effect brightens the multi-tiered Jamboree Cafe. The chairs, sea, sand and sunset pastels are the resort's common theme.

A motif of hunter green sets Duke's nightclub apart from the pastel themes of the resort. Even the columns behind the bar are green. The burgundy-colored woods in chairs and tables are the only relief.

A lovely outdoor setting in the Jamboree Cafe is backgrounded by a tower in the Spanish style so much a part of Southern California. The terrace looks out on 26 acres of lush landscaping.

WESTIN KAUAI

Location: KAUAI, HAWAII, USA
Hotel Company: WESTIN HOTELS & RESORTS
Interior Design: HIRSCH/BEDNER & ASSOCIATES
Architecture: LAWTON & UMEMURA
Photography: MILROY/MCALEER

The Westin Kauai is unlike any other hotel on the tranquil island: it's monumental, with 854 rooms, 10 restaurants and lounges, and numerous public spaces.

The restaurants range from the casual poolside area to the sophisticated cliff-side Inn with its 200-degree panoramic view of the Pacific Ocean. It has light pistachio walls, slate floors, hand-woven carpets, and shuttered windows.

The artwork selected for the Kauai was guided by its grand scale, unlike its smaller sister resort on the island of Maui. The designer commissioned artisans to recreate some remarkable ethnic pieces.

In the huge reflecting pool, for example, life-sized white marble horses are showered by the geysers from waterfalls. These horses, weighing nearly 100 tons, were reproduced in China and shipped to Kauai by boat.

Public areas are enhanced by romantic lighting, and several styles of chandeliers were specifically designed for ballrooms and restaurants. Exterior chandeliers for the pool walk were particularly critical: they had to be visually beautiful, but able to withstand the island's occasionally forceful ocean breezes.

The suites have marble floors and custom area carpets, but there are three different schemes; this multiplicity of motifs helps ''scale down'' what otherwise could be an over-imposing structure.

The Kauai, with a multi-million dollar art collection purchased in Asia, proves big can also be beautiful.

Exquisite Oriental vases mirror the vertical line of the columns that frame the Colonnade Pool.

The Inn on the Cliffs is sophisticated dining, but takes full advantage of 200-degree island/ocean panorama with a wall of French doors.

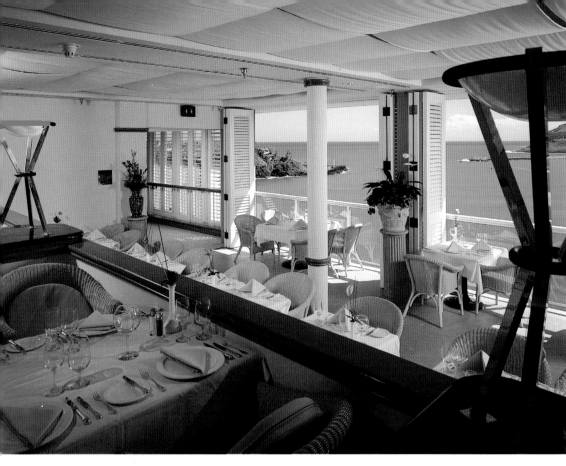

The wickered elegance of Prince Bill's restaurant affords an overwhelming view of the glorious Pacific Ocean.

A stunning, custom-designed chandelier and huge, museum-quality tapestry overlook the round-columned porte cochere.

INN AT SEMIAHMOO

Location: BLAINE, WASHINGTON, USA
Hotel Company: ATLAS HOTELS
Interior Design: THE CALLISON PARTNERSHIP
Architecture: THE CALLISON PARTNERSHIP
Photography: DICK BUSHER/ROBERT PISANO

The goal of the design for the Inn at Semiahmoo was, perhaps, not to look "designed at all."

"We and the owners wanted to capture the feeling of a treasured private home. We used a diverse selection of wallcoverings, upholstery materials and furnishings to achieve that fact," says Charlene Nelson, principal-in-charge of design on the project for Seattle-based Callison Partnership.

The lines of the furnishings were kept fairly low in most areas of the hotel to reflect the residential tone and mirror the building's architecture. Situated on a site at the end of a mile-long sand spit that once served as a cannery, the hotel's exterior was limited to four stories and plays up views of the open sea to the west and Mt. Baker to the east.

Hemlock and pine were used extensively to expand this natural but upscale atmosphere. A two-story fireplace is a visual focus for the lobby, but it is also a design motif. Forty of the hotel's 200 guest rooms have fireplaces. Depending on their location in the hotel, the rooms pair fresh white wicker with a refreshing blue, or reach into a deeper palette of bronze and green. Whatever the colors, however, the rooms feature overstuffed furniture and warm hints of pine.

Accessories complete the residential environment. They are not big-impact, priceless monuments. Rather, they are the small but important items found in homes—antique books, clocks, botanical prints and nautical-inspired brasswork.

With its overstuffed furnishings and roaring fire, this could easily be the living room of a fine home—exactly the affect the designer sought for this deluxe resort.

A large space is brought
down to more residential
proportions thanks to the
beautifully-framed central bar
and the varied heights of the
seating areas—all of which
give easy sightlines to a
panoramic view.

Four different color schemes
were used in the guest rooms
to emphasize their
individuality. This one recalls
the blend of deep burgundy
and blue with pine—a timeless
mix used throughout the
hotel.

MARINA BEACH HOTEL

Location: MARINA DEL REY, CALIFORNIA, USA
Interior Design: BARRY DESIGN ASSOCIATES
Architecture: SKIDMORE, OWINGS, & MERRILL
Photography: MARY E. NICHOLS

Though the immediate surroundings of the Marina Beach Hotel are the waters of a lovely marina, this 300-room property is not far from a busy airport or competitive luxury hotels. For this reason, the design environment had to be complete in every detail.

Exquisitely detailed and etched beige marble, generously used throughout the public spaces, sets the stage. Though the lobby has the imposing columns of traditional hotels, they look anything but "old world." In some cases, they reach through open squares to extend into upper floors. The seating around them is arranged more informally, and uses a monochromatic beige fabric for the seating, but a surprising muted plaid on the back.

A decidedly Oriental influence appears in delicate vases and artwork that enhance both the lobby and corridors. Of contrasting style but equally high quality are the crystal chandeliers and heavily-carved etched glass used in the public spaces.

These themes must carry through the entire area to underscore its relaxed resort appeal, because the hotel has very few internal walls. Changes of floor treatments, from marble with area rugs to patterned carpets, offer one solution for defining spaces with different functions. Strategically placed plants and seating arrangements also help direct both the eye and traffic flow.

Lobby seating becomes more intimate when the focus is placed on an elegant table accented with a single Oriental bowl. This grouping also is screened off from the bustle of the hotel by delicate greenery and the elegantly displayed Chinese horse sculpture.

A monochromatic color
scheme creates drama in the
Grand Ballroom. But, to add
excitement, the design has
mixed different textures and
coordinated the inset stripes
of the carpeting with the
pattern of the ceiling molding.

The temple-like entry to the Stones specialty restaurant gives patrons just a glimpse of what they can expect. The repeated design of the pediment draws the eye to a trompe l'oeil work at the far side of the room.

PETER ISLAND
HOTEL & YACHT
CLUB

Location: PETER ISLAND, BRITISH VIRGIN ISLANDS
Interior Design: XANADU DESIGN LTD.
Architecture: ROGER DOWNING & PARTNERS
Photography: DAN FORER/PETER AARON ESTO

It is surrounded by lush, rolling hills and azure sea. It is far from "civilization." It is island living with modern, even deluxe amenities. That's why guests go to Peter Island Hotel & Yacht Club, and why designers decided to bring the natural beauty and casual lifestyle of the islands indoors.

This is an environment in which ceiling fans and rattan are as appropriate and unaffectedly elegant as crystal chandeliers and mahogany would be in a city center setting. Rather than citified

marble, the walls are faced with a mosaic of stone. Plants of varying heights and density draw the verdant outdoors into the hotel.

Seating includes a practical but eclectic range from soft strapping on chairs in areas open to the weather, to bright stripes and prints for areas protected from the weather.

"This area has heavy salt air, high humidity and frequent rain. There are limited facilities for cleaning and maintaining furnishings. All of this meant

that we had to be very careful in our specifications, and choose items that could withstand the climate and be fully serviced by local firms," says Linda Selzer, of Xanadu Design, which has offices in New York and the British Virgin Islands.

But these limitations did not hamper design. Certain types of wood, as well as glass and tile, fit all these criteria and added to the design impact of the hotel.

These strapped chairs and tile-topped tables can withstand the island's heat and humidity without sacrificing tasteful design.

Use of natural materials in the guest rooms emphasizes the remote location of the resort. However, its soft seating and innovative storage insure that no "creature comfort" is overlooked.

Primary brights bring a tropical energy to the public spaces. Seating groups are small and intimate, with comfortable chairs, to encourage guests to relax and linger.

When rain keeps guests from enjoying the outdoors, they can sink into this bright sofa and take in the scenery vicariously through this charming trompe l'oeil tile work.

The outdoors come indoors by placing plants on either side of this patio door and sheathing the chairs in natural tan wicker.

Though dramatic beams angle upward, the line of this room is kept low and residential with the horizontal sweep of the casegoods and mid-rise backs and wide seats of the chairs.

Interior Designers

Photographers